Super Student
Happy Kid !

by Sally D. Ketchum

Summer Island Press
Williamsburg, Michigan

Copyright © 1995
Sally DeBolt Ketchum

Published by Summer Island Press

Library of Congress Catalog Card Number: 95-69769

ISBN 0-9647160-0-3

Additional copies may be obtained by sending a check payable to
Summer Island Press for $11.20 (includes postage) to:

Summer Island Press
P. O. Box 279
Williamsburg, MI 49690

. For your convenience, an order form can be found at the back of
this book. Special rates are available for educational fund-raising.

Printed in the USA by

MORRIS
PUBLISHING

3212 E. Hwy 30
Kearney, NE 68847
800-650-7888

This book is printed on recycled paper.

What they're saying about *Super Student/Happy Kid!*

From pre-school teachers who are using the tips on teaching listening, to college students who want time to socialize, from professors who teach teachers, to 7th graders taking tests, Super Student/Happy Kid! *readers are captivated by the usefulness of its advice and tips.*

"Each time in my undergraduate years that I faced a major project, assignment, or stressful situation, Ketchum's tips and philosophies were right there: simple, powerful, and highly applicable.

"She places emphasis on being happy as well as being successful which makes success that much easier to achieve. Further she teaches self-reliance and instills confidence which allows each student to achieve his maximum."

-- Ian Doten, B. S. University of Michigan
   Wayne State University Medical School

* * *

"As I read *Super Student,* I could not help but remember how impressed I was as I observed Ketchum's masterful interaction with students in the classroom. Her writing in *Super Student* is an incisive and instructive reinforcement of her performance as a classroom teacher and as a teacher of teachers."

-- Paul Oberle, Ph. D. , Professor Emeritus
   Teacher education, Central Michigan University

"Sally Ketchum's 'Play hard, study hard, but don't mix the two!' philosophy helped me at Boston College and beyond. It is an idea I keep handy to accomplish more and enjoy more in life."

--Jason Evans, Boston College
The University of Michigan, B. A.

* * *

"Ketchum's insights helped me succeed at Western Michigan University as a student and as a teacher. I used them to study at the University of Seville in Spain, and I use them now while teaching high school. They are sound advice."

--Michael Braun, B. A., M. A.
Teacher, Portage Northern High School, Kalamazoo

* * *

"Ketchum has the background and keen professional insight needed to provide parents and students with valuable information on how to study and compete in today's schools."

--Dr . Elmer Peterman, Superintendent
Elk Rapids Schools

* * *

"Ketchum writes with a grace and elegance that has won her hundreds of diehard fans. Her writing shows an obvious love of teaching and talent for doing it creatively. She is bubbling with ideas of how to do anything better.

--Anne Stanton, Editor and writer

"I've watched Mrs. Ketchum unveil leadership potential in students from all walks of life. She introduces them to new philosophies and attitudes that are vital to successful leadership and demonstrates unique techniques to improve specific skills.

--Leah Cole, Kalamazoo College
Leadership Forum
State of Michigan Summer Institutes (gifted ed.)

* * *

"Ketchum's Red Hot Tips not only help me get 4.0's in class, but they also help me approach my professors, keep my classwork organized, and give me ideas for socializing."

--Samantha Brown, 19
Northwestern Michigan College

* * *

"Great ideas and well presented--*clear* to our cluttered minds. My favorite section was *Quiet*."

--Cheryl Wall, young mother

* * *

"The tips are wonderfully helpful. I think all kids can use them. I especially like the category about tests. The test tips will help kids who don't have much experience most of all."

--Lauren Wilkinson, 7th grade
Cherryland Middle School, Elk Rapids, Michigan

"If all students and parents of school-age children were to read and take to heart the advice in Ketchum's *Super Student/Happy Kid!*, American education would get all the reform that it needs. Ketchum reminds us that intellectual and moral life cannot be separated, and that the subjects we study are called disciplines for a good reason: through exercise and self-discipline it is possible to acquire the virtues necessary for successful study. This book is chock full of advice on how to accomplish this, and Ketchum has wisely expressed her counsel in a variety of ways so that her ideas can be understood by students at every level from K-12."

--Dr. Robert Felkel, Professor of Spanish
  Western Michigan University

For Thad

who taught me about Innisfree

Preface

When I began teaching, I stuck to my subject, driving straight toward student understanding and appreciation of the material under study. When other ideas interrupted, remembered experiences, tangents, or new ideas piggy-backed onto the subject under discussion, I put them aside for later use.

At times I could recall these often valuable ideas; sometimes I could not. Even when I could recall the ideas, they lacked their initial freshness and vigor, and they seemed like afterthoughts.

My practical solution to this dilemma was to supply students with Red Hot Tips books, notebooks which they had to have open and ready to use at all times. From then on, when an important idea--on or off the subject--came to mind, I stopped. "Red Hot Tip!" I'd say, and I'd share the sudden insight.

The Red Hot Tips opened a kaleidoscope of experience to me and to my students. They felt free to volunteer Tips of their own. Thus we carried on through the lessons of the day, but frequently stopped to consider and explore the tangential ideas which often became quite important, themselves.

Red Hot Tips books became popular. Students took them off to colleges and photocopied them for their roommates. Both students and parents requested that a collection of tips be written in book form, and thus *Super Student/Happy Kid!* was born.

I hope that *Super Student* captures the spirit of intellectual motion in a good classroom: young minds, fresh ideas, intellectual curiosity, and the grand mix of student perspectives and sensibilities.

"Whirl is King," as Aristotle said. And I believe that is as true in scholarship as it is in genetics and in life. I suggest that you keep a special notebook for the whirl of ideas you encounter throughout your education.

Sally Ketchum
Williamsburg, Michigan

Foreword

In times such as these when there are calls for reform and innovation at all levels of our educational institutions, it is worth noting that some fundamental elements of the educational process will not change. This book assumes these unchanging elements as its foundation:

... The student who is learning well almost invariably is happy, and has a positive self-image.

... An intelligent approach to learning gets better results for the energy and time spent.

... The education of children and young adults should never be delegated entirely to teachers and schools. The importance of the parent/mentor cannot be overemphasized. Learning is a holistic and whole-life experience.

... All students, including pre-school youngsters, should be afforded the awakening of curiosity and accorded the satisfaction of knowledge and the mastering of skills.

This book addresses these elements from a very practical rather than theoretical perspective. It is loaded with specific suggestions and advice based on years of real classroom teaching experience and parenting.

Parents who use this common-sense approach to the nurturing of growing students should be encouraged to embrace the spirit of this book and put their own minds to work in furthering the learning effort.

Students who use this book will find tips and good basic advice for a lifetime of learning.

--Dr. Cecil G. Miskel, Dean and Professor
  School of Education
  The University of Michigan

CONTENTS

Self Empowerment

The Facts of School Life

Study Skills

The Three R's
Reading, (W)riting, & (A)rithmetic

The Cutting Edge

The Higher Self

Appendices

Contents by Alphabetical Order

Self Empowerment

ATTITUDE

"They can do all because they think they can," writes Virgil in *The Aeneid*. If teachers hear any one line repeatedly, it is, "I can't write, give a speech, do algebra, etc." Students should banish such negative attitudes and make their philosophy, "I can, I will, I'll work, I'll learn, etc.".

▲ *A Word to Parents*

Parents must pick up the banner of role models of attitude. Sadly, many parents excuse their children with their own defeatist attitudes: "Well, I wasn't very good at math myself." or "We really don't read much at home." Two ideas for parents to improve their children's attitudes are: 1. Monitor children's attitudes toward school and encourage good ones, and 2. Adopt a contagious, "I think I can, I think I can..." attitude yourselves.

▲ *A Word to Teens*

They do it in sports; you can do it in academics: PSYCH YOURSELF UP! I suggest an athletic training practice to enhance academic attitude. I call it *Affirmation and Visualization*. Here's how it works: Write down one academic goal, e.g. "I will write a 1,000 word short story." Then write five positive, true statements related to the goal, e .g. "I read short stories." "I can invent characters." " I know what a setting is." and so on. This stage is *Affirmation*. Re-read these statements once during the day, and once before you go to bed. The next stage is *Visualization*: Think of the story finished, your work done! Think of someone you respect reading it, intrigued. Now, relax and think positively. Train your attitude.

4 SUPER STUDENT/HAPPY KID!

▲ *A Word to Middle Schoolers*

It is always fun to be the best, to be tops! Yet, sometimes people who get all A's and the teacher's attention seem to be stuck-up or conceited. Still many bright kids have good attitudes. Think about the kids in your class who are smart and who do good work, but are also very kind to others. They have the right outlook. How do they act? How do they feel about school work? You might want to try three attitude boosters: 1. Do your very best at school. 2. Share your talents by helping someone else. 3. If you appreciate help you get from the teacher and classmates, thank them.

▲ *A Word to Young Students*

Think of school as your "job." Your mother and dad have jobs that are special to them. School is your special job. When you think of school work as your job, other parts of the school day, like recess, lunch, friends, and parties, become play time! This play and fun helps you to do well on your school work.

▲ *Pre-School Thought*

Parents, have you ever seen a person who is afraid of dogs pretend to like a dog? It's funny, isn't it? The dog will not respond to the person because he senses fear. If dogs sense true feelings, certainly youngsters do. Try not to engage in activities with your children unless you are truly relaxed, loving, and peaceful. A child is better off playing with toys in a crib or playpen than being held by a person who is angry with the world.

Red Hot Tips

☞ The first step to gain a positive attitude is to expect a good change in your work.

☞ You do not have to *be* as you feel others *see* you.   Many students have come to me, saying, "Everyone thinks I'm a jock, and I really am interested in school!" I coach these students to see themselves as scholar/athletes, and their school work improves dramatically. This not only expands their reputations, but makes them feel good and true to themselves.

6 SUPER STUDENT/HAPPY KID!

BEHAVIOR

O tempora! O mores! Cicero bemoaned the times and the manners of his age. Two thousand years later, things haven't changed much. However, man is a social creature, and therefore he continues to use good manners to ease relationships among people, including relationships in school. Manners, proper behavior, and grace--all of which are thinking behaviors -- are conducive to student success.

▲ *A Word to Parents*

Several battles of manners rage within 10 miles of my home. A nearby high school is polarized over hats. Should boys be allowed to wear caps in class? In town, some citizens charged teens with rude behavior and loitering. The issue went to the City Council. Younger children who come to my door asking for donations or selling treats for scouts, school, or church, take my money without a thank you. Perhaps a third of our children write "Thank you" notes. Yet, good manners make life easier for all, and good manners in the classroom make learning not only more pleasant, but more effective.

▲ *A Word to Teens*

All your behavior sends signals. Check your facial expression for peacefulness and accessibility, your posture for body language that signals alertness, and your actions for manners. Retrieve the words "Please" and "Thank You." In an academic atmosphere, behave in an adult manner. Office personnel only put their feet on desks on TV. Bankers do not blow bubble gum bubbles. Consider your behavior an aspect of your academic demeanor. Being cool is fine, but being cool academically is really smart.

▲ *A Word to Middle Schoolers*

Good citizenship, being calm and polite in class, is cool. If you have trouble being good for long times, practice being good for shorter times. Look at the clock, and do your very best for 10 minutes! Another good idea is to practice changing your moods. If you get the giggles, enjoy them for a moment, and then practice getting serious and down to work again. If you are feeling sad or bored, try thinking (or doing, if possible) things that are happy and upbeat.

▲ *A Word to Young Students*

Make a mini-poster to list the kinds of good manners you like to use. Put it in your notebook or school desk where you will see it. Make a new poster, changing the list if you like, every month.

▲ *Pre-School Thought*

During playtimes with very young children, being "formal" is sometimes fun, and it lays ground for more complicated manners later in childhood. A parent can playfully address the child as "Mister Matthew" or "Ms. Jessica" to send messages of respect even if the child is too young to understand the titles. Physical signals of manners, exaggerated bows, salutes, handshakes, or smiling nods send wonderful signals.

Red Hot Tips

☞ Thank your teacher after a particularly good class. Be specific in your praise. "You read that poem beautifully, and the poet's emotion really hit me!" or "You explained Problem 17 so clearly. It was like taking apart a clock! Thanks!" You will inspire your teacher immensely and feel good yourself. Try it.

☞ Read about and practice ACTIVE LISTENING (See Appendix D.).

☞ If the front of the classroom were stripped of chalkboards, posters, and other paraphernalia of teaching and replaced with mirrors--wall to wall, floor to ceiling mirrors-- education would be reformed!   Think about it.   Stop occasionally during the school day to look at yourself in this imaginary mirror.

FLEXIBILITY

Heraclitus, a Greek philosopher in the Classical Age (500 B. C.), thought that trouble and change were the two natural conditions of the universe. How true today, more than ever! Although we try to limit trouble in our lives, we are usually more successful accommodating change. We've learned that rigid positions and beliefs are seldom workable in life. They do not work in scholarship either.

▲ *Word to Parents*

If you asked my students to give my battle cry, many would say, "*Nothing's set in cement!*" Indeed. Today we are driven by goals, task commitment, critical paths, and sadly--at times with our tunnel vision--only the light at the end of the tunnel. Ironically, what may save us is not drive, but flexibility, the ability to change and accept change. Children's growth and the accompanying changes demand parental flexibility. Encourage flexibility in your family's routine and in family members' thinking. (SEE CREATIVITY.)

▲ *A Word to Teens*

Goals and stick-to-itiveness (task commitment) are important; yet there is nothing, nothing whatsoever, that is "set in cement"-- that cannot, somehow, in some way, be changed. Relationships can be made, broken, improved, or allowed to deteriorate. When you feel burned out and stuck on a plateau, you can change it into a launching pad. If the class is *truly* impossible, you can drop it. If, while finishing a paper, you decide it is awful, then trash it, and start over. Stand up to negative peer pressure if you feel tempted, or change your peer group. The courage you will feel will carry you over the embarrassment and temporary loneliness. Brave kids do this! Folks on the cutting edge are the first to see change coming. In fact, they make it happen! (See LEADERSHIP.)

▲ *A Word to Middle-Schoolers*

Ask your teachers and parents if you can make some changes. Sometimes we are happier with small changes. Try something different. Decide where you would like to sit, and ask the teacher if you could change your seat. Some ideas of things to change (with permission): bedtime, snack foods, color of your room, hair style, sports, type of books you read, Saturday activities, furniture arrangement in your room, and how you eat breakfast.

▲ *A Word to Young Students*

Changes in our lives, especially big changes like moving or parents divorcing, bring many different feelings to us. Some are good, and some are bad. When a change is bothering you, write down a list of the good results. Use large, capital letters. Beside it, list the bad results, writing smaller with lower case letters.

Your list about a new class and grade might look like this:

New class	Old class
NEW FRIENDS	will miss Alicia
NEW TEACHER	liked old locker
HIGHER GRADE	liked old schedule
GET BEST LUNCH HOUR	miss Mr. Garcia
JEFF'S IN CLASS	liked sunny windows
START LONG DIVISION	near drinking fountain
NEW COMPUTERS	work was easy

▲ *Pre-School Thought*

Introduce changes (in food, routine, activities, people in the child's world) carefully, but *do* introduce change. While repetition teaches desired behavior, change keeps life interesting.

Red Hot Tips

☞ Decide when change is or is not valuable.

☞ Bend an index card in two to make a self-standing little sign that says, "Nothing's set in cement." Put it where you can see it as you study. Think about it! Challenge ideas when you read. You might end up understanding why you agree! Try a new pattern of writing to make your point: Instead of the usual *deductive* pattern, try writing *inductively*-- giving the supporting points, then the main point (See THESIS and THINKING ON PAPER.)

☞ When you write, consider all your drafts material for change. Even the final draft might be re-written later. Put your best work away in a drawer for three months or longer. Then, take it out to revise it once again. Many excellent writers do this.

HABITS

This book could be titled "Good Habits." That title would clearly represent much of the content. However, I didn't like it since habits are so boring. A habit is somewhere between things we occasionally do and addiction. Habits are personal behaviors we have because they are easy or comforting (Several bad habits are very comforting!), and yet they are generally under our control while addictions are not. Management of habits is perhaps the most important study tool of all.

▲ *A Word to Parents*

By providing your children with a *place* to study, by carving *time* from family activities for them to study, and by giving *encouragement* in the form of proper study tools (including snacks), you support your children's habit of studying. There is one parental habit that is an exceptionally good influence: It is reading. Let your children *see* you read. Have magazines and books of several types in the household. Each child should be allowed a subscription to his or her favorite magazine. Excellent children's magazines are published now. Don't worry too much about *what* kids are reading. Take pride in the fact that they are readers.

▲ *A Word to Teens*

Habits are behaviors we sometimes repeat unconsciously. If we repeat a behavior often enough, we will do it unconsciously, automatically. Bad study habits include TV (above all), shooting the breeze with friends too much (long telephone conversations), sleeping too much, and mixing other activities with study time. Establish the good patterns of study recommended in this book by first disciplining yourself to do things right; then follow through by repeatedly doing them, and finally, stick to the good habits you've acquired. This includes daily study and efficient study. Review the contents of this book and list the chapters most helpful to your current actual study habits. Review those chapters. Good study habits will not only improve your work (and your grades), but they will make life easier and give you more time for sports, leisure, and a full social life.

▲ A Word to Middle Schoolers

Set aside two or three periods of time each day for certain activities. For instance, you may want to get up earlier to practice your instrument or go through dance or exercise routines. You might want to declare the first half hour home from school utter "goof-off and relax time." You will find that you look forward to these times! You might want to finish your homework right after dinner. Your routine might depend on whether you like to do things in the morning or evening. This is something you should think about.

▲ A Word to Young Students

Try to do your homework at the same time every day. Have a reward when you finish. This might be a snack. It might be changing into your grub clothes. It might be playing with the cat or walking the dog! Make a favorite mark or put a sticker on your calendar each day you finish your homework.

▲ Pre-School Thought

Routines are reassuring. Happily, they also enable parents to surprise children by breaking routines. (See FLEXIBILITY.) Both parent and child need routines and the pleasure of breaking them! A break in the routine may solve problems. Eating problems: Hold the peas for a while. Change the order of presented foods. Sleep problems: Move the crib or bed with respect to the monster closet or the window with the lovely view. Expanding the quiet period before bedtime often induces sleep. A considered change in the parents' routine is often refreshing to adult life, also.

RED HOT TIPS

☞ Personalize your study place, and your study routine will become pleasurable. Use colors, equipment, posters, furniture that especially please you. I know one "A" student who puts on a favorite thinking cap. Another drinks his favorite fruit drink and calls it "Study Juice." Psych yourself up! Experiment with different music instead of the same old stuff. And try quiet, too (See QUIET.). Don't surround yourself with sentimental things or pictures of boyfriends or girlfriends. This is time to put your heart into head work!

☞ Learn a new word a day. You can warm-up for study this way. (See PREPARATION.) You might want to get a word-a-day calendar; you might want to go through the dictionary. Use that word several times the next day, and be conscious of the word as you use it in the future. It will become "yours," i. e. enter your spoken vocabulary.

☞ Make a habit of rotating the posters, bulletin boards, and art in your room as a museum curator does.

☞ We have three vocabularies. Our reading vocabulary, the largest (We think we know the word when we see it.). The spoken vocabulary, next. The smallest is our written vocabulary, words we use confidently when we write. Make a habit of bringing words into your spoken and then written vocabulary.

HUMOR

"Even the Gods love their jokes," Plato wrote some 2,300 years ago. The Gods have had their jokes on man; however, man has used humor to ease diplomacy, charm his beloved, and spice literature throughout history. Today, humor is used in therapy, in entertainment, and in every good classroom. Humor in all its forms is one of life's great natural pleasures, and its place in scholarship is apt and well deserved.

▲ *A Word to Parents*

Goal: Increase humor in the household. Read the comics and discuss them. Did you know most geniuses love the comics? Encourage joke telling which is, after all, a practice of story-telling and speech! Parental puns are wonderful--they are a legitimate target for your kids' groans and disgust. Humor is the No. 1 way to diffuse the embarrassment and awkwardness of goof-ups. Warning: Humor is one thing; teasing is another, and parental teasing is dangerous.   Children are sensitive beings, and they experience teasing as cruelty, not as fun.

▲ *A Word to Teens*

Look up humor in a thesaurus. Use a dictionary to examine the different kinds of humor. Get a good text on writing or a dictionary of literary terms and study the devices in creative writing that contribute to humor: understatement, overstatement, paradox, incongruity, etc. Put more humor in your life, in your speech, your work, and your thoughts. Aim toward *wit* which is intellectual. Avoid being ludicrous or just plain silly (stupid). You can also use humor for serious purposes, such as in college application essays!

▲ *A Word to Middle Schoolers*

Humor makes a good hobby. It is free and it is fun. Make a scrap book of cartoons you like or of your favorite comic strip. Ask your librarian if she recommends any humorous books. Writing funny poems is a good way to learn creative writing. When someone tells a joke well, compliment the teller on the way the joke was told! Become a specialist: Collect dog jokes or tongue twisters. A simple tip: Smile often.

▲ *A Word to Young Students*

Having a good sense of humor means knowing how to have fun. Memorize knock-knock jokes. Get a book from the library on drawing cartoons. It's easy! Buy a notebook and make your personal "Fun Book." First give it a funny name. Make sections in it for different funny things. Some ideas are: A page for funny words. A section for jokes. A section of funny faces from magazine ads. A section where you can draw clowns. A section of funny family photographs. Your mom, dad, or older brother or sister may have some ideas, too. Share the fun.

▲ *Pre-School Thought*

Humor is so important to growth that most early learning and picture books have elements of humor. As you read to your child, *editorialize*. Explain the humor. "So very many animals in Red Fox's canoe is funny." "Look how big he is! Look how crowded they are!"

RED HOT TIPS

☞ Learn the vocabulary of humor. Remember: "Specific is terrific." Was the line in the play *witty*? *Droll*? *Fanciful*? *Satiric*? Or a marvelous *malapropism*?

INDEPENDENCE

Once I taught a fair-haired lad who depended, all through high school, on his hard-working best friend to do homework for both of them. The lad got through high school with good manners and good grades. Although he flunked tests frequently, this good boy was given the benefit of the doubt: His homework was always well done. He arranged to room with his friend at the fine state university. However, there self-sufficiency was required; he left at mid-term. Moral: Eventually, we must become independent to be successful.

▲ *A Word to Parents*

Knowledgeable parents realize that children mature in different ways and at different rates. Nevertheless, fostering independence while knowing how much freedom to allow is difficult for even the best of parents. Parents feel their responsibility to guide and protect their children, while the children naturally seek independence. A rule of thumb is helpful to strike a balance: Be aware and care. Know what is going on, but allow the child suitable independence.

These are areas that you might consider for various age groups: TEENS: Spending money, social life, and schedules. Certainly allow independent thinking as the teen engages in thought about politics, religion, love, and the meaning of life. Yet, there are things to be firm about. Besides sexual activity and substance abuse, *be firm about work*. Obviously work is a worthy experience for children. However, *if at all possible, limit working to a reasonable number of hours. Too many teens sacrifice school for work, usually to pay for cars.* PRE-TEENS: Middle schoolers should have moderate independence in choices of hobbies, music and dance lessons, friends, and clothes. YOUNGER CHILDREN: Elementary age children can choose, with minimal guidance, types of free play, foods, reading matter.

Use reason, be flexible, but encourage independence. For instance, for teens, a curfew is the last resort. If the teen-ager abuses the freedom to keep reasonable hours, then parents should set a curfew.

▲ A Word to Teens

Few teens need to be told to seek independence--from parents, teachers, and home and school rule. "Let freedom ring." However, you can examine your habits and routines for independence in other areas. Do you do your own homework? Do you join an activity because your friends do? Do you have a totally bad day because a best pal is absent? Can you be happy and productive by yourself or with new kids at times? Discover your patterns of dependence and independence and evaluate the possibilities. Make a habit of consciously sticking up for yourself on a small choice occasionally--for the sake of independence. Stick up for seeing a certain movie, for instance.

▲ A Word to Middle Schoolers

Ask your parents to call a family meeting to discuss ways that you can be more independent. Make a list of decisions that you might be allowed to make for yourself. Perhaps these will involve clothing, practice or homework times, or week-end activities. Make a list of things you want to do that will encourage self-reliance. Such a list might include: A week's visit away from home, a camping trip, a museum visit, a five mile bike ride, and so on.

▲ *A Word to Young Students*

Ask your parents if you can have friends from school over to join your neighborhood playmates. Make a list of five things that you want to do all by yourself. Make sure they are things that you really want to do. One young friend of mine wants to read in the library without his mother "right there." Another wants to choose his friends' Christmas and Hanukkah presents by himself.

▲ *Pre-School Thought*

Childproofing the home is obviously important to safety and health. It is also critical to the child's development. Think about it: Once the baby can walk, he lives in a world of constantly being told "No! Don't touch!" At the same time, all the child's instincts for development urge him to touch, to poke, to explore. Encourage this independence and help make healthy exploration possible: Childproof. Also choose picture books that show success. One example is, *The Little Engine that Could.* Maurice Sendak's *Where the Wild Things Are* shows that adventure for the child hero can end safely. Select your child's books in this light. You'll find librarians to be very helpful; they enjoy using their expertise for things more challenging than stacking books!

Red Hot Tips

☞ Study for important exams alone, then with a group, and then review alone once again. You will gain from brainstorming followed by making independent evaluations. Younger students: Find a special study place and always use it. Try studying alone. Spend some time figuring out a problem before you ask for help. Also do your homework at a usual time each day. See how often you can announce, "Homework's done!" before your parents ask.

INFLUENCES

We are all influenced by external and internal forces, including other people. Further, we all influence others for good or for bad. Awareness of such influences is the first step to controlling them and also part of making conscious choices and living deliberately.

▲ *A Word to Parents*

Parental guidance of children can be viewed as a pyramid. First, the broad base: Point out influences on your children, both good and bad and discuss them (See LISTENING and Appendix D.). If parents listen actively, the child might solve the problem of a negative influence alone. If it persists, unresisted, try firmer guidance by setting up a system of counter-balance and rules.   Try substituting a healthy-but-desired option for the unhealthy-and-desired one. "You cannot go to Florida with that gang, but you can spend the $400 on in-line skates and equipment." The last resort (and most pointed policy) is an unequivocal ban or taboo on the offending influence, and if necessary, the practice of "tough love," which translates, for teens, into "You're grounded!" or for 18 year olds and older, "Shape up or ship out!"

▲ *A Word to Teens*

You check the car's oil.   Do you also give yourself occasional motivation checks? Do you want to do something because: Someone else does it? Someone will *like* your doing it? *You* want to/should do it for yourself? Consider these reasons. Perhaps you will change your mind, perhaps not. Nevertheless, making conscious decisions strengthens us all and makes our lives richer. (See INDEPENDENCE and SELF-

ESTEEM.) Definite bad influences: Drugs/alcohol, smokers, advocates of sexual activity, doom-saying pessimists, airheads, deadbeats, and television. List five adults in your life who are role models of some sort to you. Under each, list their finest qualities in your judgment. Think these lists over now and then, and adjust them.

▲ A Word to Middle Schoolers

You've all heard the "Just Say No to Drugs" slogan. Staying drug/alcohol free is critical to being a good student and healthy person. Saying "No!" to other bad influences is important, too. Do not be tempted by sex experiences, illegal activities like shoplifting, or dishonesty, like lying to parents or teachers. Be brave about speaking up to friends to say, "No, I don't do that."

▲ A Word to Young Children

The world is full of wonderful things. You feel good when you have a true friend, or eat a fine dinner, or see a play or circus. If someone tempts you to do something you do not understand, always, always check it out with a parent or teacher. If someone suggests doing something mysterious, don't! Find out about it first. And of course, don't do anything you *know* is illegal, unhealthy, or cruel.

▲ Pre-School Thought

Control your youngster's experience. Avoid bad influences yourself. Parenting pre-schoolers is demanding. Keep company with positive folks. Complainers and whiners make poor company. They sap energy and the natural optimism from parents who need these things to raise children. This is especially true if the family is expecting a child. Remember, too, from birth on, the child is heavily and constantly influenced by his environment. (See CREATIVITY and QUIET.)

Red Hot Tips

☞ Study with studious students in places that have an academic atmosphere. Consciously pick a couple of teachers or successful students as role models. Sit in desirable places (Ask to change!) in class and in the school library. Just working in a private library carrel is a powerful, positive influence. If your library does not have carrels, try a corner. Do *not* sit in rear corners in classrooms. If your last name begins with "Z" and you often seem stuck in the rear of the room, discuss the situation with your teacher. Most teachers will let you move if you ask politely.

☞ Don't censor your reading. Get a Great Books Foundation (Chicago based) list from your library, and read widely. Different points of view will influence you in different directions, and you will end up being well-read, open-minded, and an independent, educated thinker!

PRIORITIES

Over dinner one night, I asked Dr. William Reader, a professor of Greek and religion at Central Michigan University, what single piece of advice he would give my college bound students. "Set priorities," he said. "If students get their priorities straight, everything else is on the way."

▲ *A Word to Parents*

1. Parents who have their own priorities straight will be the mainstay of a strong and confident family. Reserve both time and means for your own leisure and self-growth. A healthy, calm parent is a good parent. 2. Be ready for surprise--even shock--as your child starts to establish priorities. This is an important step to maturity. Keep an eye on how your child manages his activities, but don't jump to immediate conclusions. A child who is neglecting reading, for instance, may be going through a surge of interest in math. These things often even out. Make television last on the list, if it is on the list at all.

▲ *A Word to Teens*

Living in a world of limits, laws, school regulations, and parental curfews naturally fosters rebellious tendencies in teen-agers. However, setting personal priorities is not making another restriction. Setting personal priorities is making evaluations and ranking activities in terms of interest, worth, and return--all worthy things. Living with a set of priorities as guidelines (See FLEXIBILITY.) is, in fact, a freedom-giving condition. In today's world, a teen-ager cannot do everything. Decide what you want to do the most. What's next? And, what can you live without?

▲ *A Word to Middle Schoolers*

Talk with your mother or dad about your having a Priority Policy. You might even suggest having a "family meeting," including your brothers and sisters. Think about yourself as a student who likes school and is very good in Subject 1, good in subject 2, and quite good in subject 3. Specialize in one physical activity outside of school, a sport, hiking, or even dog walking, but try others. Specialize in a hobby, painting, piano, or dancing, too, while you check out other interests.

▲ *A Word to Young Students*

Sometime early in the day, at breakfast or on the school bus, ask yourself: "What is important to do today?" Your answer might be, "Taking a spelling test." It might be, "Finishing a book." It might be, "Remembering a special assignment at school." Think of three things you want to do well today, and do them well!

▲ *Pre-School Thought*

A funny cartoon strip showed how a mother got a reluctant child to dress in snow clothes by letting the child set priorities. "Which do you want to put on first? Boots or mittens? Which do you want to put on first? Hat or scarf?" Of course, the child wised up, but the lesson is apt. Give the pre-schooler choices. Priorities not only guard against wasted energies, they actually energize efficient action. Starting early sets the pattern. Priority setting is making choices.

RED HOT TIPS

☞ Start your homework with a plan. Get supplies ready: juice, notes, books, etc. Budget available time. List work by priorities. If you don't finish the list, don't worry about what you did not do. Worry is counter-productive.

REWARDS

Modern Education 101: *Reward works better than punishment.* The carrot on the stick is a classic motivational technique. Along with it, as every school child knows, there are also treats, perquisites, plums, and dividends for good work.

▲ *A Word to Parents*

The key to encouraging your child's academic growth through rewards is to think first, consider each reward carefully before it is offered. Does it fit the achievement in size and scope? Is it a reward the child wants or one you think he should have? Does it have an element of care, whether that care takes the form of love, appreciation, or nurture. Importantly, a reward should not encourage greed. Remember: Character growth comes first. Surprise awards count double: A favorite dinner for a science fair good job, though it didn't win a prize. Flowers on opening night for a modest role in the play.

▲ *A Word to Teens*

Don't expect rewards from others. Sadly, the world is too busy, and folks like teachers are among the busiest. You will encounter (especially in college) teachers who say, "I do not praise; I *expect* good work." Surely, at times you have done fine work, even 100%, and had it returned without even "Good" written on it. When you get into this situation, reward yourself! Prepare to reward yourself for the completion of a project, test or task by planning to sleep in, buy an album, or barter to get out of chores. Always, reward yourself after a success or good effort, whether or not it succeeds, even if it is only a contemplative moment for a self-pat on the back! Imaginative and free rewards work, too. Remind your parents of your good work: "Hey, Dad, talk for five minutes about my good job!"

▲ A Word to Middle Schoolers

A big distinction to understand and to keep in mind is the difference between who you are and the jobs you do. Always, you are a worthy person, even when you do a poor job, or do something bad. Remember that you get rewards, whether grades, treats, or favors, because of the *job* you did on a task, not because you are you. You are a good person, whether or not you receive a reward. Another interesting thought: One reward good students get is proud parents!

▲ A Word to Young Students

Sometimes rewards are not fair. There will be many times that you feel that you did the better (or even best!) job on school work. Yet, another classmate gets the good grade, the attention from the teacher, or the best place on the bulletin board. When this happens, think: "I know I did a good job, so there is something I do *not* know about why the other person was chosen. Perhaps he or she needed attention and love right now."

▲ Pre-School Thought

Although routine and consistency are important pre-school influences, surprise and delight foster creativity, appreciation, and positive attitudes. Vary rewards: Verbal rewards, happy changes in routine, returning a favorite toy that has been put away, and yes-- even food, nourishing, or perhaps if not and the child's favorite, a very small portion. A reward should be a delight!

Red Hot Tips

☞ Mark "bonuses" in your homework plans. These might be a soda after 20 pages, or a jog after your have finished your chemistry. Younger students might have a treat when they finish their homework. Study breaks aren't just rewards; they are very necessary re-charging periods, especially in high school and later. Fresh air makes an excellent reward!

☞ Reward others for their kindnesses to you. Such rewards come back in multiples! Remember the Golden Rule.

☞ Think of some person in your life who is doing a good job. Get a small reward, a funny card, a candy bar, etc. and save it until you think the person is having a busy day or a problem. *Then* give the reward!

☞ Parents can, at a minimum, reward children's successes by actively listening to the child's account of the deed or event.

The Facts of School Life

CALENDAR

We hear much now about seasonal disorders. We get the blues and the blahs without enough sunshine. We suffer holiday depression, cabin fever, etc. To combat seasonal woes, it's smart to look at our personal calendars. What happens around our birthdays? Do we expect too much? When do we start or end big projects? How do we feel about these things?

▲ *A Word to Parents*

Take a tip from the colleges. Terms like *freshman rush, sophomore slump*, and *senioritis* show important relationships between time periods and student success. Look over your children's seasonal patterns. Times to consider are the start and finish of sports activities, holiday distractions, the child's favorite season of the year. Distractions, such as prom time are large problems in high school, science fairs or recitals in middle school, and all major holidays in elementary schools. Report card time is always stressful. Realizing the effects of calendar is a step of parental support. Remind your children ahead of time of the expected busyness and talk this over with the family.

▲ *A Word to Teens*

As soon as you finish reading this section, get several sheets of paper and brainstorm all your thoughts about your calendar for the year. (SEE THINKING ON PAPER.) On one sheet, list good days/times of year, bad days/times of year. On another fill in a September to June calendar with general events (sports seasons, school play, debate season) and specific days, field trips, Homecoming, commencement, etc. On a third, fill in dates and seasons special to you, birthdays, family spring vacation, etc. Take as many notes as you can, and study them (Re-read them and think about them.). Then: 1. Plan your study life sensibly, and 2. Understand that calendar affects your work. Get the term paper done before spring vacation. Don't have your wisdom teeth pulled before an ACT or SAT test. Think and plan ahead. (SEE PRIORITIES.)

▲ A Word to Middle Schoolers

Your school work will go better if you remember that busy times are also exciting times. During team tryouts or before big class trips or holidays, plan to slow down at times. (SEE QUIET.) Keep a calendar in your room or where you do your schoolwork and highlight busy days with a bright color. This will remind you to have your school work and projects in good shape so that you can be relaxed and "cool" during exciting times.

▲ A Word to Young Students

Holidays, whether Halloween or your birthday, are sometimes happier if you remember two words: *Little* and *Slow*. Keep your very favorite activities little and slow: Bake fewer cookies, but more slowly and carefully decorated. Take rests between activities, and do things more slowly so you can enjoy them. Don't get overly excited.

▲ Pre-School thought

The children's section of a good store (also good catalogs.) suggests ideas to make seasons special for toddlers. Bundled infants and toddlers can go out in snow in carriers. The latest distribute the child's weight around the parent's hips. Try strollers. A child can enjoy outdoors in a heat wave properly shielded from sun. Be creative about improvising less expensive ways to gain the benefits of the more expensive equipment. Aim for "a happy child of all seasons."

Red Hot Tips

☞ There will be times (calendar) when doing everything on your study list is impossible. (SEE PRIORITIES once again.) Do what is most important, and plan to do the rest later. Take the penalty without worry. One student had major quizzes in physics, chemistry, and AP biology the same day. He decided to study physics and chemistry and take a lower grade on the AP biology quiz. He reasoned: He would make up the lost progress when he could, and do well on the official AP biology test at the term's end. He did just that, earning hours of university credit.

☞ Even older children expect special birthday days. Ask any teacher. Further, it's true; 16 is an important birthday!

☞ Be aware that new things are exciting and therefore invigorating: The start of the school year, new teacher, new sports season. Also be aware that the blahs are normal during long times between vacations, during year-long courses, and long tests. Work hardest during these times. Beware the sophomore slump: Plan interesting courses then. N. B. Make a personal battle plan with stress busters to fight senioritis. Some colleges withdraw acceptances if a senior performs poorly his last high school term.

COMPETITION

The slogan, "No. 2 tries harder," is successful advertising because people know it's usually true. How hard does No. 3 try? And what of No. 4 and 5, or the poor fellow who is last? Students are in the thick of competition. It is an ever-present element in school, whether for grades, membership in honor societies, or even to be teacher's pet. A good principle: Emphasize healthy academic competition, and avoid the destructive kind. "Over-caring," caring too much, is the term some physicians give competition when the student loses perspective and becomes stressed.

▲ *A Word to Parents*

Listen for overtones of competition as your children talk. Support their eagerness and goals by emphasizing their progress, productiveness, and success rather than their rank. Your support during their mistakes or when someone else "captures the flag" is critical. One family that does a fine job of parenting frequently reminds their children, "There is always someone smarter (richer, more creative, etc.) than you, and you are always smarter (richer, more creative, etc.) than someone else. Enjoy your gifts; think positively, not first." When a child loses, or comes in behind his expectations, support with the attitude that one benefits from mistakes, from challenge, and even from loss.

▲ *A Word to Teens*

I am always secretly relieved when I hear that a student has lost a 4.0 average. To me, that means the student can now relax and concentrate on what he is learning and enjoy getting an education. (See GRADES.) When you feel your competitive instincts rise, stop and consider what is fueling them. Is it love of chemistry, or is it jealousy over Jesse's neat lab reports? On the other hand, drumming up some friendly competition often relieves the doldrums during a long term. Make conscious choices concerning academic competition, and make them for the right reasons.

▲ *A Word to Middle Schoolers*

As you become young men and young women, your sports and your school work become more competitive. Competition is good when it helps to prepare you for high school and presents interesting challenges. Competition is bad when it lets you down, making you feel bad if you do not do well. When you lose a race, misspell a word in a bee, or miss a prize on a project, look back at your performance. Were you a bit lazy? Did you rush at the end? A winning attitude is being able to say, "I did my best job!" A best job is always possible, even if coming in first is not. Find out what "personal best" means when running track or cross-country.

▲ *A Word to Young Students*

Would you race an automobile with your bike? Would you race a turtle to school? Would you enter a cooking contest with a restaurant chef? These contests would be stupid. What kind of contests are smart? Can you think of some? Here is a puzzle: Why would a teacher give a prize to one student for reading 10 pages and the same prize to another student who only read 5?

▲ *Pre-School Thought*

Children of this age are in the "Discovering the Wonderful World" stage. They need toys to learn, space safe to explore, and they need self-esteem. They do not need competition.

Red Hot Tips

☞ As a track or cross-country runner aims for a personal best at the race, build your study habits and attitudes toward the test, the exams, term paper time, etc. Aiming for your personal best is healthy competition. Don't be a grind about this, though. Keep your perspective realistic.

☞ There is nothing more intellectually elegant than fair-mindedness in academic competition.   It leads to open-mindedness,   grace,   and   altruism.   Man's   highest accomplishments rest in these virtues.

☞   Read   Aristotle's   "The   High-Minded   Man"   from   his *Nicomachean Ethics.*

EXTRA-CURRICULAR ACTIVITIES

The activities outside the strictly academic life of school are important to student life. Such activities vary from school to school (what is offered) and from individual to individual (personal preference). The key to intelligent handling of extra-curricular activities is to use common sense, keep healthy perspectives, and maintain some control.

▲ *A Word to Parents*

What's coming up may sound like sports-bashing, therefore I preface my words with this: My family has been actively involved in youth baseball, basketball, floor hockey, gymnastics, swimming, softball, track, cross country, and especially ice hockey. However, this book is about scholarship; and my opinion, based on years of experience, is that *there is too much emphasis on sports in schools.* The over-emphasis in high schools (especially in small high schools) is damaging, and it is trickling down to middle and even to elementary schools.

Parents should call for athletic programs at intelligent rather than fanatic levels. When ten year olds spend week-end time needed for rest and leisure, for quiet introspection, on busses or in motel rooms for sports tournaments; when eight year olds have unnecessary, expensive, elaborate uniforms; and, when six year olds get large trophies for team membership, the program is fanatical. Further, in many such cases, both the schools and the families have tight budgets. I am not against sports. But for academic success, *academics must come first.* Too many people fall apart at 20 or 30 because they have been led to believe that glory on the court or field is lasting. With an occasional exception, other activities like band, debate, drama, interest clubs and honor societies are usually kept in perspective. In summation, students should enjoy athletic participation, but the emphasis in school should be on studies and learning life-long skills.

▲ *A Word to Teens*

The hero/superman junior of the school (a charming, honest, true-blue kid) came to me privately one day in tears. "Stress," he said. "Fell in love."

"Lovesick? Stress from love?" I asked. "Not from the fact that you're class president, and you co-captain varsity basketball, have the lead in the play, and chair the ecology group, belong to three honor societies, not counting debate, band, and student council? Let's talk about it," I said.

Healthy, well-balanced high schoolers usually can handle young love (not sex). Extra-curricular activities are something else. Focus and limit. If you want to be a student first, studies must come first. Integrating work and play, school and activities, personal interests, and free time into one young life is challenging. However, it is possible. Establish priorities, including time for personal growth and rest. A review of these sections will help you: CALENDAR, PRIORITIES, QUIET, and SELF-ESTEEM.

▲ *A Word to Middle Schoolers*

More and more choices are open to students as they go through school. During middle school years, kids usually feel busy playing in one sport per season and joining in one or two activities or clubs at a time. Add one thing at a time to your schedule to see how it goes. Always speak up if you feel stress. Tell your parents if you feel too busy or stressed out. Ask your parents, "Please listen to me carefully." Never think or feel that you'll be disappointing your parents or letting your coach down. Parents are there to care, and coaches are there to coach. You deserve the help! If things go well, if you still have extra time and energy, add another activity. Activities should be fun.

▲ *A Word to Young Students*

Sports and clubs are very interesting. Talk with your parents about things you can join that will be a pleasure for you. Activities should be fun.   There is enough serious work at school.   Can you start your own club with neighborhood friends? Try it!

▲ *Pre-School thought*

The old rule of thumb, "One guest per year for birthday parties." usually works. However, it may allow one too many for *play*. A two year old, for instance, plays best with only one friend. This is also a good philosophy for activities. In keeping the policy of a safe, relaxed environment for the toddler to explore, one activity at a time is a good idea.

RED HOT TIPS

☞ Practice blocking out (forgetting) extra-curricular activities when you study.   This is what concentration is, and *concentration can be learned*.   On the other hand, you might want to choose an extra-curricular activity to enrich an academic pursuit. Being in the school play will help the debater's speaking skills. The application of knowledge learned in school can be surprising. A physics student may want to use his knowledge of leverage as a member of the wrestling team. Such a physical sport is also a total change of pace from sitting in class. Think your routine through; consider your goals; and make conscious choices.

FAILURES/BLOCKS

The higher a student climbs up the ivory tower of education, the harder he falls if he slips. Early failures are considered part of childhood. Further, modern schools try to take the sting out of encountered problems such as holding a child back a grade in elementary school. However, there is little to cushion the sixteen-year-old's shock over a low ACT or SAT score or a letter denying the 17 year old admission to the student's desired college. Proper handling of failure, mistakes, and learning blocks should start early and be a serious aspect of academic training.

▲ *A Word to Parents*

Before you evaluate your children's success in school, you might do well to check out the competition. Competition does not necessarily mean classmates. (See COMPETITION.) Check out the teacher (See LEARNING STYLES.), the course (content, methods, level of difficulty), the text, the requirements for diploma, college admissions, etc. Knowing the territory and the rules will enable you to intelligently and confidently support your children when they meet failure head-on, languish on a plateau, or encounter a writer's block.

▲ *A Word to Teens*

Once, during an extreme family crisis, I consulted an intelligent, compassionate minister and also a highly respected psychiatrist. Although the psychiatrist charged more, they gave me identical advice: "Be confident, go forward, and act upon what you know is right."

I said, "How can I do this? I'm a basket case, a nervous wreck."

They both said, "Write down a plan for action, follow the plan, and proceed by rote." Deliberate, rote action will move you forward, out of crisis, off the block, and free you from stress. This works. Write down a plan to read when you confront the crisis (or it arises once again). Then when you have trouble steering your course, you can switch to automatic-pilot, the plan. RULE: When stuck, go back one step. For example: Learn the writing process and follow it. If stuck, back up one step. Go back to thesis from outline. Go back from proofreading to drafting. Math: Re-do the last problems you did correctly. Review the last chapter. Musical snags? Repeat drills, practice exercises, then approach the problem anew. General ennui? Boredom? Learn something new. Plateaus are just one part of the learning journey. Eventually your mind feels rested and speeds (or bumps) along to the next station.

▲ A Word to Middle Schoolers

Everyone makes mistakes. Smart people look at mistakes and the sometimes lousy jobs they do as opportunities to learn more or to improve. To do this, analyze (See: HIGHER LEVEL THINKING SKILLS.) what the mistake or failure is. How did it happen? Fix the broken parts. Learn the skills that failed you. Think through the project, game, or activity again, and visualize doing it well.

▲ A Word to Young Students

When we make mistakes we sometimes feel that everyone is looking at us. We feel really stupid. Neither one of these things is true! Think about sports. If we strike out, the next batter is up, our team or their's. Everyone looks to the next fellow. If the goalie slaps your shot away, play goes on instantly!

▲ *Pre-School Thought*

The feeling of failure has no place for pre-schoolers. Parents have the responsibility to see that the child's environment is conducive to successful experiences. These balance the small failures the pre-schooler has in "learning through experience." Such an environment encourages a healthy optimism and security while the child explores his world. Given this, he will grow and develop at his own pace. Simply, children this age do not fail. The baby falling while learning to walk is practicing "Walking 101."

RED HOT TIPS

☞ Make a list of specific goals for each particular subject (See ATTITUDE.) Star those that you know are attainable. Do these first. Now-- you have succeeded! Work toward the other goals on the list.

☞ Not everyone can win the race. One person will win, and one will be last. Blocks can be overcome; plateaus can be used as launching pads. Expect to occasionally fail a task, flunk a quiz. Don't let it throw you when it happens! Back up, get on task, and carry on!

☞ Sometimes intelligent children do poorly because there are family problems such as alcohol abuse or divorce. Signs of such problems are when a seemingly bright child neglects homework and is careless, disorganized, or prone to daydreaming. When such symptons arise, the child should have strong support and probably counciling from parents and teachers.

GRADES

There is a strong movement in American education toward holistic grading. Such grading evaluates the whole student. It assumes that all aspects of student education are interdependent. Examples of these aspects are potential, opportunity, progress, performance on individual tasks, effort, etc. This emphasis on the whole may even mean there are no letter or numerical grades. The reasoning behind holistic grading is that it is not only fair and more humane, but that it actually promotes learning.

▲ *A Word to Parents*
Letter and numerical grades often tell you more about the teacher than about the student. Is the teacher a hard grader or a pushover? Does he teach an exact science or a class where grading is necessarily somewhat subjective, as it is in creative writing or art? Inquire about the school's grading policy, and ask your children's individual teachers how they grade.

Unfortunately, grades for the college bound are important. Nevertheless, do not overemphasize grades. Learning is the goal, and learning will produce high scores on SAT and ACT tests. These scores are "grades," too. Don't overreact to a low score. The tests can be re-taken, and the highest score is counted. Sometimes honesty will counter the impact of an occasional low grade. One student I taught was admitted to West Point although he had a low score on the English section of the SAT. An admissions official wrote me to ask about the low score. I said (honestly) that the student was qualified, and he simply had had a bad test day. He was admitted and is now doing well at the Academy.

▲ *A Word to Teens*

All students know that grades are not always fair; yet, everyone wants high grades. To raise your grades (along with using the other advice in this book): 1. Ask how your teacher arrives at grades. Understand what the teacher wants. 2. Consider your learning style and the teacher's learning and teaching styles. (See LEARNING STYLES.) Obviously, the teacher will teach using projects and lesson plans which fit his learning style. Adjust accordingly. As far as your assignments go, do them "his way," but you may be able to supplement assignments with some extra work "your way." I taught one student who always added art to the required written report. 3. Work steadily; do daily work daily. 4. Periodically ask about your current grade, but do not pester.

▲ *A Word to Middle Schoolers*

Make learning your goal, not high grades. Sometimes you will receive grades that are unfair. Don't let these upset you. You might ask the teacher to explain the low grade and try to understand what the teacher wants. Perhaps sometime you will get an unfair grade that is high! Encourage your parents to attend teacher-parent conferences. Invite them to come.

▲ *A Word to Young Students*

When you get your report card, talk about it with your parents. Tell them what work you are doing--reading, skits, problems, projects--subject by subject. Sometimes ask your teacher what she likes about your work. Ask, "What words describe my work?" Also ask what you can do to improve.

▲ *Pre-School Thought*

Parents should take care to always comment about the performance or "job" a young child does. They should take care *not* to broadside the child with "Bad girl!" or "Naughty boy!" Even very young children need self-esteem strong enough to survive doing bad jobs now and then. A pro-active approach, correcting the mistake, substituting proper behavior for undesired behavior usually works and lays ground for understanding approval. Later, approval will be high grades.

RED HOT TIPS

☞ Before you study, ask "What is expected in this assignment?" (See WHAT and WHY.) How important is the current task? Just daily homework? Is it an important lab report or language essay? Keeping track of your homework assignment and noting such information should be a routine part of studying.

☞ If you want to master a difficult subject (and get a high grade), take easier subjects along with the difficult course. Such a schedule might be: AP biology, algebra II, art, American history, physical education, and modern short stories.

☞ If you read the biography of any great person, you will find that he or she has had a bad grade now and then. Develop the ability to laugh at a complete disaster while you learn from it.

SCHOOL SUPPLIES

Don't be "penny wise and pound foolish." Fine quality in frequently used supplies (scissors, ruler, etc.) is a good investment. A stapler that jams frequently is a life-long nuisance!   Trash it. Innovative supplies encourage creative thinking.

▲ *A Word to Parents*
The paraphernalia of academic life is part of the desired atmosphere for the serious student.   Building a scholarly physical environment helps the student become the scholar. The process should be on-going: an addition to the student's scholarly equipment each birthday; small gifts, e. g. stationery, good   pens,   classical   CD's,   for   encouragement; a medium gift, e. g. an *Oxford Companion* to his favorite humanities subject or *Van Nostrand's Scientific Encyclopedia* for a budding scientist); a large gift of a bookcase, desk, or file as   a   gift   for   starting   high   school   or   upon   a   major accomplishment. If affordable, a computer should be introduced to the child's home study environment as soon as possible.

▲ *A Word to Teens*
Take time to think through school supplies. Do not depend on schools with tight budgets to supply you with optimum materials. Buy a separate spiral notebook for *each* subject in serious colors and one in fashion, neon, or camouflage to mess around in. Tearing a sheet out of your biology notebook to write a hall note undermines your scientific attitude. Spiral notebooks lie flat and free your hands to turn pages, doodle, and gesticulate. Test pens at an office supply store, and buy the kind that feels good to use, something special that makes you

aware that your work is special. Get colored high-lighters. (See NOTES.) While you are there, look around at the offerings to see what you can use for schoolwork. Be creative! Think future: What will you use in college? Look through supplies at a college bookstore for ideas. Your ideas and work are precious and individual; good supplies will remind you of this. Throw out or re-cycle beat-up things.

▲ A Word to Middle Schoolers

Talk to your parents and decide what you need for each subject. Use a separate notebook or loose-leaf section for each subject. Decide what you need for your desk or study center at home. If you do not have a desk, keep all your study supplies in a special box. Ask for a $15 "fund" to buy special items when you see them, items that interest you: Tape that's sticky on both sides, special pencils, stickers, and graph paper. Buy things that make you feel good about school work and use them! Refresh supplies at each term's start.

▲ A Word to Young Students

Find out what supplies the school will give you. Then ask to go on a special shopping trip to a discount mart to buy your extra supplies. You may pick up freebies if you ask your mother and father to be alert for supplies which might help you! Make your supplies special to you. Can you get most things in your favorite color? Can you find things with your name or initial on them? Be sure to have a bookbag or case to hold everything, and put your name on it neatly. Be proud of your school things. Have some special things at home, too.

▲ Pre-school Thought

A parental visit to a good office supply store will inspire many ideas for unstructured, open-ended, imaginative activities. Simple colorful file stickers are better and much less expensive than comic/TV character stickers. Colored papers and large-sized (easy to hold) markers and poster boards inspire art. Poster board also makes disposable bulletin boards. Or, create a giant book from those the child makes! Page-sized, plastic magnifying sheets are safe and encourage early science. An art supply store will have "newsprint" pads, sheets of large and inexpensive paper for student artists of all ages. Large pages open the mind and free the imagination. Ask the store's clerks who are familiar with stock for more ideas.

Red Hot Tips

☞ Get ready for study by physically running a check-through of supplies, as a pilot checks his plane before taking off. Do you have everything you need (including soda and snacks)? Is everything in the right place? This nit-picky activity actually helps you make the transition from leisure to study. Don't knock it-- make it a habit!

☞ Start and use an organizer, whether it is an inexpensive, pocket organizer or an expensive leather file center. Keep calendars, to-do lists, addresses, phone numbers, and lists of ideas. Journalists call idea notebooks *morgues*.

☞ For fun, be an antique/historical buff. Get a pen holder and try to find some old-fashioned pen points. Find a slide rule (Ask older relatives!) and learn how to use one to amaze your friends and possibly your math teacher! Incorporate all kinds of fun into your supplies: Beauty, charm, wit, and belly-laugh humor (glow-in-the-dark ink?)!

STRESS

Stress is the ultimate cause of many modern ills: health problems like heart failure, stroke, and depression and social and family problems like substance abuse, child, wife/husband, parent abuse, divorce, etc. The list goes on. Never before in history in a secure and powerful nation have young people been so stressed. Seventh graders discuss college admissions, and mothers say that eight year olds are stressed by loneliness or peer problems. In school, social life, problems of acceptance, athletic competition, and of course, academic challenge are all major stressors.   Further, there is the pressure that the individual student puts upon himself.   To improve student success, students and parents have to confront the issue of student stress.

▲ A Word to Parents

The teeter-totter position of the teen, one minute confronting adult issues, the next being treated as a youngster, is difficult enough without the added burden of the trickle-down of parent stress. In the last decade, more and more student conversation has revolved, not around the problems teens are having with their parents, *but the problems of the parents:* parental drinking, fighting, lack of money, or social problems. Middle schoolers are now quite familiar with adult issues like divorce and infidelity. Parents must remember that children not only need adult guidance, but they also need protection from stress and worry. A simple tip: Schedule and preserve time just for your children; ideally there should be one-on-one time for each child, too. Encourage stressed children to slow down; and when they seem ready, to focus on one or two things.

▲ *A Word to Teens*

You could write the list of stresses for me. One Detroit high school did. Recently, teens there started to take a stress test and ended up throwing it out and brainstorming a huge list of teen stressors that weren't even on the test! Welcome to the 90's.

Tips to minimize stress include: Talk--to your counselor, friendly adult, or friends. Talk things out. In a crisis, find the area's teen crisis center. There are also good books out on teen stress. Ask your librarian. Study the behavior of adults you admire. How do they handle stress? Slow down, cut back. (See EXTRA-CURRICULAR ACTIVITIES and SELF-ESTEEM.) When you feel that you're "losing it" and "don't have your act together" examine your perspective. Are you expecting too much of yourself? Focus on what is important (See PRIORITIES.). Schedule breaks and leisure, and follow through. Fresh air and exercise are major de-stressors. Be realistic about your eating habits. Young women, especially, slip easily into bulimia and anorexia when stressed. Believe this: Drugs and stimulants don't work. Keep a list and note what stresses you.

▲ *A Word to Middle-Schoolers*

In spite of all the troubles associated with growing up, adding a year at each birthday, is a neat feeling. Yet, *"Don't grow up too fast!"* is good advice, even if it is sometimes hard to understand. You have a clear right to your young adolescence, to play, to be silly, to feel free of adult pressures. These years are important. Smoking, sex, drugs, and other temptations have no place in the life of middle-schoolers. Kids who are experimenting with these things are not only growing up too fast, they are very wrong.

▲ *A Word to Young Students*

Have you ever gone through a cafeteria line and taken too many things because everything looked so good? Taking on too many activities is easy to do, too. In one day at school, you will do many different things. Make your week happy by concentrating on perhaps just one sport or hobby or lesson after school. Be sure to have enough play time. Simple games, like Tag, Red Rover--Come Over, Kick the Can, and Bloody Murder are fun! Ask your mom and dad about games they remember and how to play them. You might be surprised.

▲ *Pre-School Thought*

Thoreau said, "Simplify! Simplify!" Robert Browning said, "Less is more!" Even Einstein advised, "Everything should be made as simple as possible, but not simpler." There is so much advice on raising children, that absorbing it all would leave no time to parent! But the advice to simplify is wise, indeed. Simplify routines and schedules, yours and the children's. Life with youngsters is hectic in itself. Plan periods of calm and free time. Free--even from play! (see QUIET.)

Red Hot Tips

☞ Divide homework into three lists: URGENT (Must do it.) IMPORTANT (Should do it.) HELPFUL (Will do it later.) Keep URGENT as short as possible; you'll feel good when it is done and inspired to start the IMPORTANT list. Work in a set period of time, breaks included. Re-make the lists after each study session and at the end of the school day.

☞ Get enough sleep. Sometimes a nap changes your outlook. Watch your eating habits. Milk products have natural relaxing enzymes. Plus, their protein is a pickup. If you are nervous or stressed, take a walk and get some yogurt or ice-cream. To sleep well, try carbohydrates before bed--a bagel is ideal. If you are seriously depressed, get help! Needing help is a human condition!

☞ "Help comes from unexpected sources." Reminding yourself of this truth is helpful. I never read Tolkien's *The Lord of the Rings* without getting this message. When all looks lost and the expected aid fails, help comes from another source. Study how various characters handle stress. (Stress and characters, incidentally, was the subject of a College Board test question.)

☞ Many people find favorite things work as de-stressors. Perhaps it is just thinking that they work that makes them work, but many successful students have an album, a favorite book, or even a food that seems to turn things positive.

TEACHERS

"Teachers are human." Teachers don't know everything, and expecting them to be experts is not realistic. You *can* expect them to know their subject areas well and how to teach the content and make students feel good about themselves and about school. Teachers also have good days and bad days. They may like chocolate or pop corn, play poker or Mozart; and, like everyone else, get head colds and parking tickets. In short, teachers are people. Remember this.

▲ *A Word to Parents*
Send five stamped, self-addressed post cards to teachers with a note that you would like a brief comment about your child and/or his work when the teacher feels communication would be helpful. Send a plate of cookies or a bag of fruit to the teacher's lounge, thanking *all* the staff, once a term. If you want to thrill a teacher, send a positive note, a *sincere* compliment once in a while. Such a thank-you note will help balance the other kinds the teacher gets..

▲ *A Word to Teens*
You are young adults now, and there will be subjects that you know more about than your teachers. You may even be smarter than some of your teachers! Nevertheless, every one of your teachers has something of value for you. Try to know enough to ask intelligent, possibly provocative questions. Play the "straight man" with your teacher as a comedian does to the top banana. Look up the term: *devil's advocate*. Some, although not all, teachers enjoy having a devil's advocate in class. Studying your teacher a little, besides the class material, is very helpful. (See LEARNING STYLES.)

▲ *A Word to Middle Schoolers*

Sometimes even teachers have bad days. Some classes or projects might be boring. Help your teacher by doing your best. Always try to be cheerful, and when the teacher has time, suggest lessons or projects that interest you. Your input helps! Instead of an apple or cookies, bring your teacher something that will help him or her teach, a funny post-note pad or an article or item that will add to the unit the class is studying. The teacher will appreciate your interest!

▲ *A Word to Young Students*

Tell your teacher when you especially like a book or a lesson. Look around the classroom and tell your teacher what things you like. Bring a favorite thing from home to share with the room. Remember you can say "thank you" for good lessons and ideas just as you do for treats!

▲ *Pre-School Thought*

Parents can use one or two "educational" words a week repeatedly to build the child's vocabulary for school. Words like *"look," "count," "find," "say," "draw,"* are good beginners. Reinforce with picture books. Keep the big basic in mind, though: "Learning should be fun!

RED HOT TIPS

☞ What is your teacher's style? Notice what he likes and try to act accordingly. Does he like quiet work? Experiments? Order? Creativity? New ideas? You might even ask! (See LEARNING STYLES.)

☞ Occasionally, ask your teacher if there is any favor you might do to help. Take down a bulletin board? Clean the board? Small favors, like straightening the bookcase, you can do without asking. These little jobs will bring big appreciation.

TEXTBOOKS

"Don't believe everything you see in print!" Even younger students know not to believe the tabloid headlines: "Two headed Elvis sighted on Mars!" Yet most students wouldn't think of questioning their textbooks, let alone doubting them. Certainly schools try to use texts that are reliable and well-written; but books, like everything else in life, are not perfect. Reading critically, evaluating as you read, is good for the brain, and such reading also helps spot passages where the interpretation of facts or literature might have incorrect emphasis, where the book omits critical facts through an oversight, or where the text might--simply--be *wrong*. Even good books have flaws.

▲ *A Word to Parents*

A fine investment is to buy copies of important text books to keep at home (Ask the teacher for the publisher's address, and write to them yourself or ask your bookstore to order the text). This can relieve the student of remembering to bring home books (and the carrying); but most important, he can write in his own books, add notes, underline, and work in the book he owns. Later, when the student is in college, high school texts will serve as excellent resources, especially for review in math, science, literature, and history.

▲ *A Word to Teens*

Learn the differences: Examining a book, scanning a book (looking though), reading a book, and studying a book. By examining a book when you first use it, leafing through pages and sections, you will discover how it is set up. Find the maps, charts, sub-heads, review sections; and you will probably also find many useful parts like glossaries and indexes. Scanning enables you to survey what is ahead and to be somewhat ready for it. You will pick up early clues to meaning and importances as your read if the material has been scanned first. Reading is careful work, and studying is re-reading, using higher level thinking skills as you interpret (See Appendix A.) and take notes. (See NOTE TAKING.)

▲ *A Word to Middle Schoolers*

Most textbooks used today are very well organized teaching tools. Learn how to use all the parts of your books. Ask your teacher to explain to the class how the textbook's various parts and features can be used to make learning easier. Use glossaries and indexes.

▲ *A Word to Young Students*

Think about what kind of book you are reading. Is it a story which the author has made up? Is it the true story of the life a real person? Look up the words "fiction," "biography," and "editorial."

▲ *Pre-School Thought*

Make the toddler an indestructible, washable bright book bag with lots of pockets (Kids love pockets, and they teach coordination.) Let the child drag it around. Keep it full of simple picture, touch-me books, and an occasional treat. A pocket for crayons for the older pre-schooler is helpful.

RED HOT TIPS

☞ Skim, scan (look quickly through) the assigned reading before you start. This will let you know what's in store, and give you time (you only need a minute) to ask questions: What could happen in the story? What scientific process am I reading about? What parts of yesterday's math will I build on?

☞ The back of the title page is called the "verso," and it contains useful information. Learn other names of book parts. You know "page." Look up "spine," "appendix," "preface," and "glossary."

☞ Young readers, don't be afraid to use books that might seem a little hard. Sometimes you can skim over words you don't know without looking them up and still get the meaning! Look up the word "context." Read this, for instance: "The church was quiet as the groom walked forward to meet his future spouse. Her gown and flowers were white." What do you think "spouse" means? Did you guess "wife?" Context helps us guess word meanings correctly, or at least our guesses are close. Read a difficult book now and then. Challenge is fun.

Study Skills

CREATIVITY

"How clever! I wish I could do things like that." How often we say this! Yet, we sell ourselves short by not nurturing our own creative instincts while we appreciate others'. While we might not eventually be able to sculpt great art or write great epic poetry, there are many ways we can increase our creativity and thereby enrich our lives.

▲ *A Word to Parents*

Parents can begin to foster family creativity in two simple ways: 1. *Recognize it.* Look for creative instincts in family members. 2. *Name it.* Label people's creative efforts to acknowledge and emphasize them. Say, "How inventive!" "Wow, great art!" "What an imagination!" "You're good at brainstorming." and so on. When our children were young, ages 5-11, we held weekly "Family Nights." The honor to choose the evening's activity rotated, and we enjoyed Monopoly nights, poker nights, some funny home movie nights. We thought we were clever parents. To our astonishment and great pleasure, however, the children's ideas clearly began to surpass ours. The kids chose such imaginative activities, our choices seemed bland. Consider: Animal Noise Night (age 7's): "I put animal names into a hat. Draw one, and go into the basement and make the animal's noise. The rest of us will guess." So there's mother, near the furnace, bellowing like a hippopotamus! Of all the nights, Invention Night (age 10's) was clearly the challenge. You guessed it! The kids' inventions, to hold up pants, to fasten papers together, to improve the fork, far out-reached ours. This is an easy, free, creative activity. Try it!

▲ *A Word to Teens*

You can warm-up your creativity just as an athlete warms-up his muscles. (SEE PREPARATION, HIGHER LEVEL THINKING SKILLS, and THINKING ON PAPER.) These activities include brainstorming and clustering (How many uses for a pop can?), cause and effect chains (stayed up too late...was tired...skipped getting gas...car ran out...late for school), etc. (See Appendix E, THINKING ON PAPER.) All open-ended thinking is creative. There is a choice of methods for many assignments. Make the most of it. Warm-up. Brainstorm a list of ways to do the work, pick the most creative, and ask the teacher's permission. You may get points on the project before you even start. Many selective universities ask optional questions in their applications which involve creativity. These are intentional hidden challenges. Attempting these questions is wise. Again, you gain points before you start.

▲ *A Word to Middle Schoolers*

There are so many good ways to be smart. The best scholar is the one who works to be tops in several ways: Use your intelligence. Start the job, stick to it, and finish it. And also do the job creatively, using your imagination in all the ways you can--through ideas, art, interesting words, etc.

▲ *A Word to Young Students*

Don't worry whether or not you are truly great in art or music or story-telling. What is most important is to make a good effort (Try hard!); and, above all, enjoy the activity. If you have fun practicing, skills will come later! Isn't it surprising that having fun can lead to learning? What a fine deal!

▲ *Pre-School Thought*

Pre-Schoolers need interaction with all aspects of their environment. Activities should include those that stimulate the senses: Water-play with cups and buckets (ALL POOL AND BATH PLAY IS TOTALLY SUPERVISED, OF COURSE) and finger painting. Play in sand or soil (Toddlers love digging!), silly putty, and play dough satisfy the toddler's urge to handle interesting materials and experience texture. Sound play is also important. Provide toys that chime, ring, or buzz and simple musical instruments. Playthings should also promote physical and emotional growth. Physical activity equipment such as jungle gyms and swings, etc.) develop muscles and self-confidence. Books, along with puppets (especially hand puppets), costume/dress-up collections, and simple theaters for role-playing, encourage language development and imagination. Large boxes make playing store or office or veterinarian possible. Avoid "closed-end" toys, e.g. Barbie dolls. They do not encourage creativity. Tip: Buy an inexpensive set (Two sets are better!) of natural wooden blocks in a standard gauge. Then check the finer toy companies' catalogs (F. A. O. Swartz, etc.) for special pieces, gothic arches, curves, cross sections, etc. that are in the same gauge. Such a set makes a family heirloom.

Red Hot Tips

☞ For pre-schoolers, keep materials simple (large crayons for gripping) and activity time short enough to sustain interest. Youngsters like to and need to paint (poster paint). Cheap paper is fine, and many youngsters even like to paint on old newspapers! A large, sturdy easel (two pieces of plywood, hinged?) is a boon. Sometimes suggest familiar subjects and stories to draw and paint; other times let children experiment without suggestions.

Large surface areas accomodate a young child's large motor skills. Hold off on the smaller, quality paper sketch pads until the youngster's fine motor skills and hand-eye coordination are more developed. The expressive impulse subsides if constrained too much.

☞ The higher level thinking skills involve creativity. Analysis: How many ways can you take things apart? Synthesis: How many different ways can you put things together? What will you add? Take away? Change? Evaluation: How and why can things be ranked, judged, or graded? (See HIGHER LEVEL THINKING SKILLS.).

☞ Keep the humanities in your schedule: art, music, literature, architecture!

DEPTH and BREADTH

With information highways, instant communication, science burgeoning with discoveries, and seemingly man's every move recorded on video tape, "knowing it all" is clearly impossible. Yet, somewhat paradoxically, there is a strong case for studying certain things in depth, certain things in breadth, and sometimes studying some things both ways.

▲ *A Word to Parents*

Sometimes students become very interested in a particular subject. They also sometimes "get hot" (find the material easy) and want to run with it, especially as they launch off a plateau, suddenly learning to read, to understand long division or the cases of Latin. While "Strike while the iron is hot!" is a good policy, at times the teacher may find that a student going ahead of the class is inconvenient. These are the times when the parent might encourage the student to dig deeper (depth), to become expert on the subject at hand while not going ahead to new subjects. With this study, the student keeps his interest alive; and, in fact, he may even enrich the class. However, if the child feels frustrated, parents might talk to both teacher and counselor or principal if they feel teachers are holding the child back intellectually.

▲ *A Word to Teens*

Education is not confined to school. In *The Education of Henry Adams*, Adams writes, "They know enough who know how to learn." Educate yourself! Look, read, wonder, and write. Find a subject that especially interests you, and become an expert. Any subject: Motorcycles, whales, jazz, or jockeys! Explore the range (breadth). How many different types and versions? Explore the depth: Get the details, the specific facts, and the histories. Enjoy being No. 1 authority in your class or school on rocks, rock and roll, or rockets. Such mastery of a subject is a wonderful feeling, and it will guide you in knowing whether or not you really have mastered subjects as you continue your life-long education.

▲ *A Word to Middle Schoolers*

You can learn about things broadly, learn about most everything on the subject. Consider "U. S. states" the subject. Example: Learn all the states in the union. This is called learning in breadth. Or, you can specialize. Example: learning everything you can about South Dakota. This is called learning in depth. Both are excellent ways of learning. By learning about South Dakota in depth, you become able to apply gained knowledge to other states. Example: If you know about Mt. Rushmore in South Dakota, you will understand that other states have their own famous monuments. You can look them up if you wish; that would be studying in breadth. The two methods work well together.

▲ *A Word to Young Students*

Pick a subject you like. Dinosaurs? Soccer? Ships? Ask for various things connected with the subject, for news clippings, books, or notice of TV shows about the subject. Small gifts like calendars or pencil mugs featuring the subject are good ideas. Tell everybody about your interest. The more you learn, the more interested you will become! (See SELF-ESTEEM.)

▲ *Pre-School Thought*

Don't worry if your child seems to play with one toy exclusively. That particular toy is serving a function at his stage of development. However, provide the option of a small variety of toys. You may want to introduce a toy similar to the favorite in an attempt to expand interest. As with toilet training and reading, "when the child is ready...." Remove toys from the toy box occasionally, so they seem interesting when returned to play later.

RED HOT TIPS

☞ When you are extremely interested in a certain subject, brainstorm ways you can learn more about it, and act upon your ideas. Try libraries-- the local public or a nearby college. Ask your teachers and parents if they know of an adult mentor near you who might guide your study. Check colleges and correspondence programs for courses you can take to supplement your studies. The University of Wisconsin and Indiana University, among others, offer both high school and college credit through such work.

☞ When studying, try using two colors of high-lighters, one for breadth (general principals, history, etc.). Mark important background with a vertical line in the margin. Use another color for depth (exact vocabulary, dates, etc.), marking the exact term. Or, work out your own system. (See NOTES.)

☞ The terms "apprentice," "journeyman," and "master" started back in the middle ages or before as men became educated, learning their skill or trade. You might think of these as you tackle subjects. Aim to be a master chemist, a master historian, and enjoy the journey along the way.

HIGHER LEVEL THINKING SKILLS

There are different kinds of thinking, and some ways are better than others. Understanding these differences is very helpful in school. A famous educator, Benjamin Bloom, labelled these ways of thinking in a classification system (taxonomy) which has become a standard and useful classroom tool for teachers. I like my students to be aware of this system also in order to understand what *way* they are thinking at any given time. Unfortunately, some far-right, ultra-conservative groups confuse teaching HOW to think with WHAT to think. Bloom's taxonomy and higher level thinking skills have nothing to do with teaching students *what* to think.

▲ *A Word to Parents*

Study the chart of Thinking Skills (See Appendix A). Make terms for the three higher level thinking skills (analysis, synthesis, evaluation) part of the vocabulary you use with your children, especially when discussing school work. Awareness of how you are thinking at various times is self-improvement.

▲ *A Word to Teens*

Good teachers use their knowledge of the higher level thinking skills in teaching. Learn about the higher level thinking skills and how to use them (See Appendix A.), and you pave the way to student success. Analysis is a key method to approach problems, to take the problem apart, whether it is a problem in the exact sciences or one in social studies or literature. Synthesis is a creative thinking tool in most kinds of problem solving. The student can put things back together in a fresh way.

▲ *A Word to Middle-Schoolers*

Learn the words: "Analysis," "synthesis," and "evaluation." Look them up in a dictionary, and practice each way of thinking once a week. Analysis is taking things apart. (What goes into the chocolate chip cookie?) Synthesis puts something back together in a new way (Add gum drops to the recipe.). Evaluation is deciding whether it is good or bad, works well or not, or why you like/do not like something. Are the cookies better with or without the gumdrops? (See Appendix A.)

▲ *A word to Young Students*

Remember a simple story or fairy tale. Divide the story according to the beginning, the middle, and the end. Make up a different ending to the story. Do you like yours better? Try this with a different story or take turns changing endings with friends.

▲ *Pre-School Thought*

Using simple directional words ("see," "take," "put," "bring," etc.) clearly during pre-school years lays the foundation for correctly understanding and using higher level thinking skills later.

Red Hot Tips

☞ Use the words involved in the higher level thinking skills, both the official term, e. g., "evaluation," and key related terms or synonyms, e. g. "convince," "argue," "criticize," "assess," etc. in your studying and *especially* when answering examination questions. Repeat words in the questions by using them and their synonyms in your answer.

LEARNING STYLES

Understanding that there are different styles (ways) of learning and that each individual has an optimal way to learn is both enlightening and empowering. There is no one way that is best for everyone, but there is a best way for each person.

▲ *A Word to Parents*

Educators classify different ways of learning as visual, auditory, and kinesthetic. They also break down these styles to various degrees and label them. One way to understand the variety is to think in terms of the child who is *visual* and learns by seeing. Another child who is *auditory* learns best by quietly listening. The third (often a nuisance to the teacher) is the child who is *kinesthetic* and learns hands on, by touching, and often dismantling, bumping, and wreaking havoc on the classroom.

These basic groups can also be broken down to *internal* and *external* styles (See Table on page 86.) They are:

Visual internal: The child likes to visualize, to remember how things looked, and he or she loves description in stories.

The *visual external* child likes TV and videos and has a keen sense of his surroundings. He knows the details of his place.

Auditory internal: This child remembers how things sound, remembers voices and music. He may even talk to himself. J. Alfred Prufrock (in T. S. Eliot's poem) has an internal learning style that is both intensely visual and auditory as his poetic internal dialog shows.

Auditory external: The child is an expert listener, concentrating easily on the speaker, and he is sensitive to the small nuances of sound and differences in language.

Kinesthetic internal: The learner needs to be at ease with his surroundings; he perceives through feelings and reacts physically to stimuli. Again, mature readers might want to study the Prufrock poem again for passages which evidence the kinesthetic internal style of learning.

The *kinesthetic external* learner is a whirling dervish. He is the athlete, the grand gesticulator, and he learns by practicing these physical activities.

Interesting studies also use such labels as: *thinking* or *feeling*, *intuiting* or *sensing*. Some educators think in terms of students who learn best by *watching*, *thinking*, *feeling*, or *doing*. All these terms have some overlap and are merely labels. Nevertheless, they give the parent and student important insight into how students learn.

▲ *A Word to Teens*
Find out about learning styles and take some simple tests to find yours! Ask your teacher, counselor, or librarians for help on this. If you strike out, try the local college library or write the School of Education at a state university for help. When you know your style, you can learn best by using it as much as possible. This knowledge may also take some of the frustration out of class when you have a learning style which is obviously the opposite of your teacher's. You may be able to make some adjustment, and at least you'll know the trouble is not because you are dumb or at fault.

▲ *A Word to Middle Schoolers*

There are many ways to learn things. Think about it. How do you learn to saw or plane wood, write poetry, or dance the Funky Chicken or Tango? Do you learn *by doing* these things? *By watching* people doing them? Or *by listening* to a teacher explain how to do them? What do you like to do best? Do it? Watch it? Or listen to learn how to do it? All are ways different people learn to do things.

▲ *A Word to Young Students*

There are many ways of learning things. Some will be more fun for you than others. Remember the things you do when school seems really fun. Try to do more things like that! If a shoe box scene was fun in art, make one for reading!

▲ *Pre-School Thought*

Does your toddler respond to toys that move or have moving parts, like push toys? (Kinesthetic child) To toys that ring or buzz? (Auditory child) Or does he or she grab the brightest toys around? (Visual child) Researchers suggest that babies as young as six months have a learning style preference. Take note!

Red Hot Tips

☞ Knowing and understanding your learning style will not only help you study better, it will also help you to organize your closets and your life, and to be more successful at work and at play. Simply, doing things your way will enrich your life and ease the way over bumps.

☞ You may or may not have success with convincing your teacher than you learn best in a style opposite his. Mr. Rigid or Ms. Perfecto will not want the kinesthetic learner moving the straight rows of desks around to pantomime Shakespeare.

However, you *can* practice your own style for homework. Go out on the balconies, kinesthetic external Juliets! Enjoy those TV civil war histories, dear visual external historians! Make your room a comfortable study place, where you *feel* like studying the wonders of theorems, young kinesthetic internal mathematicians! To each his own!

Learning Styles Table

	Visual	**Auditory**	**Kinesthetic**
Internal	Visualizes, likes how things look	Remembers sounds, voices	Learns feelings, reacts physically
External	Likes TV, is aware of surroundings	Good listener, hears well	Likes to be active, athletic

LISTENING

"The time has come," the Walrus said, "To talk of many things...." And though classes may not deal with cabbages, kings, or pigs with wings, classes are talk time, indeed. Since the teacher does most of the talking, the key skill for students is listening. Sadly, listening is the one skill frequently neglected. Even if listening skills are taught, in the end the burden is very much on the individual. The student must become a good listener.

▲ *A Word to Parents*

There are periods of childhood (Examples: Terrible two's and the traumatic teens) when children are deaf to parental instruction, pleas, and even pleasantries. When children "Don't want to hear it," you might try writing your message (clearly, simply, and unemotionally) and delivering it to your child. When all else fails, you have one recourse: Turn the tables. You must be the listener. Listen, listen, listen, and listen! You will be setting the example, and the child will know you care.

▲ *A Word to Teens*

Read about *active listening*, repeating back to the person nearly exactly what he said. (See Appendix D.) This allows the speaker to clarify or expand his thoughts It also lets you, the listener, handle the material (study it) a second time. You can try a version of this technique when listening to your teachers: 1. Listen to what is being said. 2. Since your mind works much faster than any teacher speaks, you will have time to put it into your own words (and take notes this way, too). 3. Use all possible senses to listen. Watch the teacher. Concentrate on hearing the material. Put it on paper. 4. Guard against thinking,

"Yeah, but...." Hear the teacher out or you'll miss things. 5. After the teacher has finished, form a question about the material, and ask it.

▲ *A Word to Middle-Schoolers*

Being a good listener is important and sometimes a difficult skill to learn. Since our minds think of things much faster than a person can talk, we sometimes have to slow down and concentrate on what the teacher is saying. We have to "hang on." Ask your parents to find some story-telling shows on Public Radio stations. The story tellers are excellent, and some of them are very famous! This activity can be much more intense and more enjoyable than television since it allows your imagination to work!

▲ *A Word to Young Students*

Most people seem to watch too much television. Some schools even have had contests to see if kids can go without TV for a week or even more! You might try to do this. A big tip: Listening to the radio builds listening skills. Also, try library story-telling hours.

▲ *Pre-School Thought*

Tell some stories to the child without pictures. Babies can, of course, hear, but they have to learn to listen. When reading, stop occasionally, and ask the child if he or she has any questions. Do strive to give interesting and thoughtful answers.

RED HOT TIPS

☞ When taking lecture notes, keep a special place on the note pages for questions. As in TV's "Jeopardy," re-phrase the material into question form. This makes review a snap. (See NOTE-TAKING.)

☞ If you simply cannot concentrate for the whole class period, force yourself to concentrate for shorter periods, even ten minutes "on," five "off." Gradually increase "on" time. Always check the notes of other students if you have had trouble listening.

☞ Sometimes you can play imaginary "paper doll" with the teacher to keep your attention. Put the teacher into a costume that connects with what he is talking about. Teacher talk/imaginary costume: Poe/Raven; math/Einstein; biology/skeleton. This silly trick will relax you, slow down your mind and prevent it from wandering off the subject.

☞ A challenge worth accepting-- Listen to the news on Public Radio (Their commentators are good; they speak correctly.) Try to take notes on the news. Comparing what you have learned/remembered with what is remembered by a family member who did not take notes will be very interesting. Doing this will not only develop your listening and note-taking skills, but will give you an edge in all your government and history courses, probably in others, too.

☞ If you have a hearing loss, keep current with your doctors and hearing aid dealers. New advances are being made every day. If you feel sad or depressed about your loss, talk to successful deaf people. I, the author, am quite deaf.

NOTE TAKING

The ability to take good notes is a skill that is used throughout life. Learning to take good notes is easy if you understand the "whys" of certain note-taking devices involving space, symbols, and content. Good notes make use of the fact that the student can look, survey, and locate the particular material he is interested in. Pages of summary are not good notes.

▲ *A Word to Parents*

Making the distinction between writing prose and taking notes encourages us to do both better. (See WHAT? WHY?) Certainly students have experience *writing* from the earliest grades. However, whether they get adequate instruction and guided practice in *note-taking* is less certain. Although it might seem obvious, the difference between writing and note-taking needs to be emphasized to students.   Too many students laboriously try to copy down everything the teacher or text says, word for word.   The purpose of note taking, of course, is to capture the kernel of meaning quickly. Elegant sentences are probably not very good notes.

▲ *A Word to Teens*

(**N.B.**, that's a frequently used Latin abbreviation for *Nota Bene*, "note well!") Learn how to take notes. Practice taking them the right way.   Start now. Use **N. B.** to start inventing your own private shorthand: Incorporate abbreviations, numbers, and symbols from the sciences, math, and music; academic notation (Latin); hearts, arrows, smiley faces; and original marks that are meaningful to you. Always put a large question mark in margin when you miss the teacher's comment, or cannot keep up, or do not understand. (See LISTENING.) Having your own system increases self-esteem and keeps note-taking interesting. Learn frequently used Latin abbreviations and how they are used ("e.g.," "et. al.," "etc."). Unless you quote a famous phrase or historic statement, *always take notes in your own words.* Doing so decreases the chance of unintentional plagiarism. (See HONESTY.) Using your own words is also a study aid since you process the ideas you translate into your words. Use plenty of space. Space lets you "see" things and allows for later additions. (See Appendices E and F.)

▲ *A Word to Middle-Schoolers*

Start taking notes when your teacher explains work, even if you are not certain how to do it. If something is on the board, copy it exactly. When the teacher talks, write down important words. You don't need to write sentences when you take notes. Notes are something like code, only notes are much easier to read. Still, they sometimes use symbols. Start now to learn more symbols. You already know some like stars, checks, asterisks (*), and dollar and cent signs and more. For fun, start some memory projects that involve symbols. Learn the Greek alphabet to amaze your friends. Or choose 10 elements in the periodic table (chemistry) and learn their symbols. Start a list of abbreviations (like "etc.") in your language notebook and use them!

▲ *A Word to Young Students*

Notes sometimes use small drawings to save time. Try *drawing* words. Drawing words like "tree" or "dog" is easy. Use your imagination to draw these: "broken," "fixed", "old," "song," and "fun." Try this game with a friend. Each should make a list to trade. Draw each other's words! For three or more friends, pass lists "round-robin."

▲ *Pre-School Thought*

Good magazines for pre-schoolers always have pictographic stories. Pre-schoolers love them. It's also fun for parent and child to make their own. Get a notebook and write a simple story about things the child knows, his dog or cat, grandma, and parents. A couple of packages of the various stickers sold and a rubber stamp or two make this project easy. Your child might start to read!

RED HOT TIPS

☞ Use color in your notes. Use various colors you like. The high-lighting markers available at office supply stores are excellent! Use each color for a certain purpose and stick to the system. A system might be: yellow = key terms; blue vertical line in margin = important passage; orange = memorize-theorem or quotation. Keep the system consistent, and it becomes an easy habit and an excellent visual guide. This is especially useful for visual learners (See LEARNING STYLES.).

☞ Never, ever--even with ecology in mind--take notes on both sides of a sheet of paper. When working with loose papers, doing so means 50% of your notes are covered at all times! You want to be able to see everything at once to survey your work. In notebooks, the blank left page can later be used for additional material or reflection in review.

☞ Buy thick, spiral notebooks. They stay flat when open, and allow you to think "SPACE." Cheap notebooks are not the way to save money. (See SCHOOL SUPPLIES.)

☞ **N. B.** Review your notes, even if only for a few minutes, *as soon as possible after they have been taken*. Your efficiency is much, much greater at this time. Further, you will remember things said or read that you didn't put down at the time. You will be able to jot down details and clarifications that you did not have time to capture at first. And, best of all, you will be studying the material the *third* time: First: When you heard/read it. Second: When you took the notes. Third: This after class review. This tip is a proven winner!

PREPARATION

Although I am considered an excellent cook, my husband's stir-fry is much better than mine. He has no secret ingredients, but he does take time for a thorough preparation: All his ingredients are out and measured; trimmed, sliced, or diced according to type; lined up in order of use. Watching him cook is a joy. His presentation of dinner is lovely, the food delicious. Consider that the preparation to study is just as important and just as beneficial. It is also simple. The Boy Scouts are right! *"Be Prepared!"*

▲ *A Word to Parents*

We know we have to have all our records out in order to do income taxes. We know pre-natal care is important to healthy births and babies. Yet, in small routines, we often neglect preparation. We dash off to shop and forget the checkbook. We pack the picnic and forget forks or napkins. Encourage a family routine of preparation just as you use "Stop, look, and listen" for youngsters crossing the street.

▲ *A Word to Teens*

Prepare for study, test-taking, or writing by giving yourself *warm-up time.* You might even consider warming up for your entire day. In fact, getting up 15 minutes earlier in the morning might give you time to relax, to think the day over. To fully awaken is a good preparation for the day. Prepare to do homework. Start to study by readying your study area physically. Remove all the stuff from your desk or table that you won't need, and get out everything you will need: books, notes, pens, etc. Make sure you have good light. Warm-up with brainstorming and thinking on paper. Prepare to write before actually starting a paper. Use sports techniques to improve studying. Stretch and warm-up before you perform. (See ATTITUDE, Affirmation and Visualization.) Don't cram for tests, you will only drive out information you know. To prepare for quizzes in class, visualize success, and view the test as your chance to show what you know. Generally, psych yourself up.

▲ A Word to Middle Schoolers

When you are given a new assignment, sit on your hands for two or three minutes. This isn't as silly as it sounds. When you sit on your hands, you cannot write. While you are not writing you can think over ways to do the work and get new ideas. If you start writing immediately, you haven't given your brain a chance to let your good ideas develop!

▲ A Word to Young Students

Check your school bag daily. Make this a habit. Do it every day before you leave the house. When you start a new project in school, start by checking to see if you have all the materials and books you will need. Once in a while, ask for new crayons and save the old ones to re-cycle as candles or art objects.

▲ Pre-School Thought

Use one rather flamboyant gesture before your child begins a new activity. For example, spread out a sheet on the floor for a minute before you dump the tinker-toys. Look at several books laid out, then choose one. Hum a little to get baby's attention before you sing the lullaby.

Red Hot Tips

☞ Try several methods of preparation for studying and for various classroom activities. Decide which works best for you.

Accept *warm-up* as the first step to action.

☞ Do your best work in the beginning. Prepare to work. Make a plan (ANY plan is better than no plan!) and stick to it. When you prepare a time budget, allow time at the end to check your work. (SEE PROOF-READING.)

☞ A simple mental run-through of the activity to be done is an excellent warm-up.

☞ The first step to prepare to study is to announce to the family that you are going to study. This means hold the phone calls, etc. (YES!) Something subtle operates when you do this. As a sleep expert says kneeling to pray signals the body that sleep is imminent, announcing study time puts a little subtle pressure on you to follow through. Try it.

PROOFREADING

Theodore Roosevelt's words, inscribed on the historic site of his birthplace, read: "The only one who makes no mistakes is one who never does anything!" Mistakes are as much a part of scholarship as they are of life. Some are inevitable, of course. However, fewer mistakes will be made if students learn and practice good proofreading skills.

▲ *A Word to Parents*

We sometimes allow our kids (metaphorically) to stay on third base instead of being parents at the plate to bat the kids home. We see that our children-students have started the book, solved some math problems, or are out the door to the library, but we get involved with other things and forget to help our students finish the job or arrive at their destination. Further, sometimes it seems as if finishing a job is distasteful to children. Parents should see that schoolwork is done, that writing is proofread, and that problems are double checked by the student. Assignments, after all, are about acquiring skills; and proofreading is most certainly a valuable skill.

▲ *A Word to Teens*

Nail down credit for your good work. 1. Learn how to proofread. 2. Do it--*no skipping*! There is always a great urge to skip that final step, checking, when a project is done. This feeling is universal. After all, we feel good about getting to the end, the last page or the final problem. We don't want that good feeling diluted by having to go over everything once again. Yet, that is exactly what the smart student does. Learn to proofread your writing three ways: SENSE? (Am I making good sense?) SENTENCES? (Are they complete? Run on?

Structured well? Did I vary the length?) WORD BY WORD? (Spelling and word choice). Also, have your work read by another person since we easily read over our own mistakes. Find proofreading symbols in a good dictionary and learn them. Review TEST-TAKING and MATH & SCIENCE for more tips. Proofreading can be thought of as that final look in the mirror before a big date: You just want to reassure yourself that you look absolutely irresistible!

▲ *A Word to Middle Schoolers*

A riddle: *When you have done the last problem or written the last word of your assignment, why is the work unfinished?* Answer: *The last part of schoolwork is to check it.* This is called *proofreading*. The word comes from journalism. Newspapers print first copies called proofs. These are checked before thousands of newspapers are printed. You can "proofread" your writing and "double-check" your math and science.

▲ *A Word to Young Students*

Be willing to change your work to make it better. Sometimes you will get new ideas. Sometimes you will find mistakes that you can correct. Teachers call this *polishing* your work. You are putting a shine on it!

▲ *Pre-School Thought*

Two proofing skills for parents of pre-schoolers are safety drills (for fire and severe weather) and child-proofing homes (poisons, electricity, appliances, etc.).

Red Hot Tips

☞ Plan proofreading time when you take exams. Proofreading *always* pays big dividends. It's tiresome, but it's also critical. Hang tough, and get it done. Grades are lowered more by lack of proofreading than by any other factor.

☞ A superior student I know proofreads her writing backwards for the last effort. Since backwards reading destroys sense, she can catch each word for spelling.

☞ Always be willing to correct or to change to improve. Even if your paper is typed or printed, be willing to make that one last change. Your teacher will not see that as mess; he will see it as desire for improvement.

TESTS

A good head with a good education, running on a good work ethic, will succeed on the job. However, usually it takes good test scores to get the job in the first place. Good test scores lead to high grades (and sometimes scholarships) which, in turn, lead to impressive resumes, and usually to productive and satisfying employment.

▲ *A Word to Parents*

General advice: Be aware that tests scores don't always indicate student progress. They merely indicate how the student performed that day on that particular test, which may or may not have been fair. Specific advice: Make certain your children study regularly. This means daily. When serious students enter high school, they will find that tests become serious matters, too. Cramming does more damage than good; discourage it, especially late-nighters. Buy several good test-taking strategy books for your children from a good (large) bookstore. Look through them and compare.   The better ones will stress thinking, estimating, and strategy rather than mere memorization. (See SCHOOL SUPPLIES.) This is even important enough to merit a trip to a city and dollars from your budget. Students should work with ACT/SAT preparation books the *summer* before they take the college board tests. September is too late.

▲ *A Word to Teens*

The best preparation for tests is to do daily homework and study as if there were always a quiz tomorrow. Test-taking doomers: Cramming, cheating, rushing, plunging in without reading directions and thinking, reckless guessing. Experts disagree about strategy short cuts. I believe most strategies to be helpful; at the minimum, they encourage you to stop and think. Some are listed in Appendix G. Proven general strategies are to:

... Budget your time for thinking, writing, and proofreading.
... Sleep and eat well the night before (pasta, carbohydrates for staying power!) and in the morning, milk products if you're nervous.
... Find directional words and use them.
... Never be the first to turn in your test.
... Visualize problems, if possible, and estimate answers, even if the formulas or numbers throw you.
... Again, nothing replaces daily study.

▲ *A Word to Middle-Schoolers*

Tests that require answers in sentences are called essay tests (or sometimes short answer tests). Sometimes these tests ask for your opinion. For instance: "Was the hobbit wise to go on a journey?" But when answers are very short, like circling a letter, filling in the blank with one or two words, or picking one of several offered answers (multiple choice), the test is called an objective test. These tests look for facts. For instance: "What was the hobbit's name?" If you have a clue or the feeling that you think might be right, guessing usually improves scores. Don't change your first answers unless you are truly sure that they are wrong.

▲ *A Word to Young Children*

It is very easy to get nervous before taking tests. Teachers often try to have projects and reports instead of tests to make school fun. If you do have a test, however, don't be nervous.

Relax, rub your hands to warm them up to write, take a deep breath or two, and work carefully. No one can take away the things you have learned. Tests help the teacher understand whether he or she is doing a good job, too!

▲ *Pre-School Thought*

How the world has changed in a generation--in 10 years! We now have early pregnancy tests at the grocery store, sonograms of baby, we-know-the-sex in the womb, and tests at birth to check for serious conditions. While testing infant development, researchers have come to such wondrous conclusions (valid or invalid) as that painting the nursery orange and playing classical music there raises the infant's IQ. They also say that learning starts at birth (See LEARNING STYLES.). Tests are ever-present in raising children, whether we like them or not. Certainly, various tests are helpful to pediatricians in their practice of good medicine. Usually, however, tests should be viewed as general guides. Pre-schoolers develop at surprisingly different rates. Special note: If kindergarten readiness testing suggests you hold your child back, do so. Legions of mothers say they are sorry they insisted that their children start kindergarten at five when tests suggested otherwise. I am one of these mothers. This is especially true for children born close to the cut-off date in your state.

Red Hot Tips

☞ Think positively. Instead of viewing the test as the teacher's means to check how much you know or if you've done your work, view it as your chance to handle the information once again, your chance to synthesize all that you know or to evaluate the facts. (See HIGHER LEVEL THINKING SKILLS and Appendix A.) Consider tests to be opportunities.

☞ Naturally you wouldn't ask the teacher for test answers. However, asking the teacher about the up-and-coming test won't hurt. He might give you tips on content, he probably will let you know the form of the test which will help you prepare, and at least, he will know you are scrambling for points!

☞ Writing essay tests means following the rules and techniques, as much as possible, of essay writing. This means follow essay structure, have a thesis (your answer in a nutshell), make an outline (plan), give concrete examples or informed opinions which support your thesis, and proofread.

☞ For very important exams that involve essay answers, e. g. English achievement tests, College Boards, or AP tests (including sciences), review essay writing techniques the week before the test. This strategy applies to the written portions of math and science exams as well. Also review making time budgets. If several solid students cannot finish the exam in the allotted time, the teacher may shorten his next exam. In upper grades and in college, however, many teachers give very long exams to stretch brilliant minds, and do not expect most students to finish.

☞ If you run out of time, jot down the core of your answers in note form. You may or may not pick up points.

THINKING ON PAPER

"Cogito ergo sum." I think, therefore, I am.   Descartes might have been right.   For, as thought nails down being, thinking on paper makes thought concrete and repeats it back to the brain.   Like many great processes, it is a simple thing!

▲ *A Word to Parents*

Thinking on paper is a good habit for all ages.   Do it yourself to improve performance and to be a role model to children.   Provide all members of the family with the tools to write in every possible place.   Place note pads and pencil by the phone, desk, kitchen counter, piano, in the garage, bedroom, (and, yes) the bathroom!   Instead of writing out all the directions to your children, diagram some!

▲ *A Word to Teens*

Two simple things to do, advantageous to practice, are 1. Doodle (Anything goes!) and 2.   Take notes in your own private short-hand. (See NOTES.) Be conscious of physically making a circle, or a list, or scatter-shot throwing out of ideas. The physical act of drawing a circle to represent an economic cycle ingrains the "cycle" concept in the brain.   Intellectually, "feel" the differences, the opposite qualities, when you place items on two sides of a chart.   For instance, try this: Fold a piece of paper in half, and let the top half represent "north" and the bottom "south."   Fill in these words: "Union," "Confederacy," "Grant," "Lee," "blue," and "gray."   You are reinforcing learning by using spatial note-taking.   When you put thoughts and ideas on paper, you have something concrete to deal with.   Some of the many useful ways to think on paper are exemplified in Appendix E. Study these ways and practice them. Thinking on paper has some surprising advantages. For instance, you can even let off steam. If a teacher (or significant other) is driving you out of your mind, write a letter, expressing your frustration, to the teacher (or friend). Be specific. Call the villain (teacher or boy/girl friend) names if you must! Then, read it with feeling, and trash it. You'll probably feel better (and no doubt have increased your dramatic writing skills). You can study better without frustration from people.

▲ *A Word to Middle Schoolers*

Start a list of symbols to use in code for fun. Use diagrams whenever you can. How many different kinds of diagrams can you think of? Diagram your family tree. Let your parents help. For fun, diagram how you imagine two friends think. Is there a machine in the head? Little people with thinking jobs? Opposing forces? An idea factory? Be creative in other ways. Chart the plot of a book with arrows. Draw in your diary.

▲ *A Word to Young Students*

Write a story for a small child that uses shapes (squares, circles, triangles) and lines (dashes, spirals, arrows) to show part of the meaning. Example: "Twinkle, twinkle, little * , How I wonder What U are?" Use shapes in your writing when you can.

▲ *Pre-School Thought*

Provide sturdy and colorful writing materials and various textures for the toddler to experience. Cover the kitchen floor with a sheet on a winter morning and let the child play with sand, fish tank gravel, or pasta in a baking pan. Let the child make marks and traces of shapes in the sand.

Red Hot Tips

☞ Visualize when taking notes and tests whenever possible. (Can you see an idea or problem represented as a list, a time-line, or a pie chart?)   Look up "dichotomy" in the dictionary. Perhaps you can make a chart to represent two sides of a problem.   Or consider, is the decline of a country a spiral or an arrow headed down? On a circle, where would you put Spring? Winter?   Birth? Death?   How would you represent your personality on paper? (See PORTFOLIO and Appendix C.)

☞ When thinking on paper, you automatically are studying because you are processing the material twice. First, you think it; and second, you re-think it as you put it on paper.

☞ When you show "thinking on paper"-type notes on test papers, the teacher is apt to give you extra credit for approaching the question intelligently. Do not hesitate to sketch your ideas, main points, or organization on homework or on a test.

☞ *Thinking with a Pencil* by Henning Nelms (Ten Speed Press) is an older book, but an excellent one.   The ISBN number is 0-89815-052-3 if your bookstore can order it.

WHAT and WHY?

We've all had the experience of going into the kitchen and forgetting what it was we wanted. What am I doing? Why am I here? Repeating these simple questions as we work and study maintains a focus that not only facilitates learning, but teaches us lessons along the way as a bonus. By definition, "studying" means a raised awareness of what we are doing. Review HIGHER LEVEL THINKING SKILLS and Appendix A.

▲ *A Word to Parents*

Help your children realize what they are doing in school and why. Talk with them with a MACRO view, about their broad range educational, personal, and professional goals. Also speak with them with MICRO views, considering the content of each class (what) and the purpose of it (why). Help children to see what is work, what is leisure, to see if one can be applied to the other, or if it would be best to keep them separate. Understanding why we do things makes our goal, the "what?", clearer. Work becomes easier.

▲ *A Word to Teens*

Study the pages on HIGHER LEVEL THINKING SKILLS and Appendix A. Just as you check the gas gauge on the dashboard when you drive, check how you are going to think when you study. Will you be analyzing? Why? To find out how many parts there are in the whole? Are you comparing two things? Why? To understand the less familiar one? To see which is superior? An occasional check of "What am I doing?" and "Why I am doing it?" not only keeps you on track, but actually enhances the learning experience.

▲ *A Word to Middle Schoolers*

Start your school work with a little warm up. Ask: "What am I going to do? Why am I doing it?" Keep asking the questions, in a short question chain, until you understand your assignment and feel confident. It works like this: What? Collecting leaves for science. Why? To compare them (How are they alike?) and contrast them (How are they different?). What? Glue them on posterboard and label them. Why? To display and explain; to learn about life systems.

▲ *A Word to Young Students*

Ask your teacher "WHAT?" and "WHY?" when you start a new project or assignment. In science, are you studying rocks (geology)? Animals (zoology)? How will this knowledge help you? In math, are you studying multiplication or division? When will you use these skills? In language arts, are you writing a short story (fiction) or a report (non-fiction)? Ask your teacher to explain the differences, and perhaps the purposes of the skills being learned.

▲ *Pre-School Thought*

Help the child to anticipate an activity with a pleasant announcement of what he is going to do. An explanation of the activity with transitional words helps the child to understand process and also builds vocabulary. "Now we'll find the coloring book, next we'll find the crayons. Let's decide what page to color?" Using specific vocabulary, tell the child what he is doing, "walking," "running," "skipping," or "jumping."

RED HOT TIPS

☞ When writing, 1. Understand exactly *what* you are writing and why you are putting those words on paper, e. g. *What?* "Now I am writing a transition." *Why?* "To provide my reader with a logical path of thought to the next issue or subject, from A to B, from indoor sports to outdoor sports."

or

What? "Now I am writing description, using a spatial pattern, e.g. the velvet chair next to the arched double doors." *Why?* "So the reader feels the rich atmosphere of the room."

☞ Look up the word "genre," and use it frequently. Making distinctions among genres means that you are going through the mental process of analysis, a higher level thinking skill, and also classification. Example: " In what genres did Poe write?" "Poetry, short stories, and literary criticism." A magazine might read, "Spring fashions seem to be in a nautical genre this April. (You'll see sailor suits and dresses with nautical braid and brass buttons!)"

The Three R's

Reading, (W)riting, & (A)rithmetic

MATH and SCIENCE

No one has to be told that mathematics and the exact sciences are key powers in any curriculum. These classes would be among the last to be cut by a financially stressed school system. Grades in these classes weigh more heavily with parents and college admissions officials. Students often take (and are smart to do so) less technically demanding and more skill and talent-oriented classes like band, typing, and art to balance demanding courses like physics and trigonometry. While some, including me, insist on the importance of the humanities in education, math and science reign in this age with its passion for technology.

▲ *A Word to Parents*
Math and science are areas that need regular, daily, consistent study. Parents would do well to see that younger students bring their books home and see that students of all ages complete and then check their daily work. Teens who take demanding math and science courses may need a study hall if the school allows such periods. They will certainly need quiet, uninterrupted time, and a place to study at home. Regular class attendance is also critical. In literature, a student may skip a Poe story and go on to the next tale with understanding; he or she cannot skip the first half of a chapter in pre-calculus or chemistry and understand the last half. Listen (See ACTIVE LISTENING.) to the child about the class and the teacher. If you feel there are problems with the math or science teacher, talk to the teacher, counselor or principal about the problems. Never hesitate to hire a tutor. Many advanced students tutor. Be supportive and encouraging. Never be punitive; punishment never solved a geometry problem nor

wrote a biology lab report.

▲ *A Word to Teens*

Math and science are big time, right? They are not only impressive on the old schedule, but the truth is: They are critical to college and career. Make certain that you understand the work and assigned material *each day before you leave school.* If you don't understand, ask your teacher for an appointment for help. In these classes, once behind, you are usually lost. If you are home sick, call friends to talk about each class, keep up. If stuck, back up and review the last problems or chapters. Re-read; review principles, theorems, and laws frequently. Make a huge, wall-to-wall blackboard in your room or in the basement. Stand and scrawl formulas and math on it like the mad scientist. Such boards are easy to make with "Masonite" (Tempered "Masonite" is about as hard as a slate chalkboard.) and specialized chalkboard paint for this purpose. Once you solve the math or science problems from working at the board, you can copy them neatly, thereby reviewing them still again, especially if you *think* as you copy. *This really works!*

▲ *A Word to Middle-Schoolers*

Math and science are important, and they are fun. Doing the work also leaves you feeling mighty good since the problems are done, and the answers are there (right or wrong). The feeling is something like being on a quiz show. This is not always true in other classes. Several good suggestions for math and science are: Finish your homework every day. Re-check your homework (See PROOF-READING.). If the book has optional problems, do them. Skim (look over) work ahead of schedule. Review DEPTH and BREADTH. Hit the library and read about Einstein's life and find out who Stephen Hawking is!

▲ *A Word to Young Students*

When you are given a memorization project, take it on. Make flash cards, get parents to listen to you recite, and learn the multiplication tables or the vocabulary of science. Make it a game. (See REWARDS.) Tell your teacher or your parents when you get behind or do not understand the work. Getting help when you need it is important. *Never* pretend that you understand something when you don't.

▲ *Pre-School Thought*

Play counting games from age two on. Reciting numbers is not counting. (See THINKING SKILLS.) Provide counting books, play finger games, give the child safe objects to count and reinforce counting with objects around the house: apples, oranges, chairs, and books. Counting activity should be kept short, no more than five minutes, even if the child is delighted. Provide geometric shapes in blocks and toys. (See CREATIVITY.) Use the classic early board games, like "Candyland." *Always support learning; never pressure the child. Learning should be fun.*

Red Hot Tips

☞ If students want a challenge which is very rewarding, they can learn the multiplication tables up to 25. This will be a life-long advantage; it's very quick for estimating.

☞ While doing homework in math or the sciences and also while taking tests, never underestimate the help that *estimating* gives you! Learn to approximate time, space, and materials. When unsure, certainly when you're lost, *estimate answers* to show that you understand the question if not the number crunching stuff. This works especially well if you can use any type of diagram. (See THINKING ON PAPER.)

READING

When I was quite young, my mother complimented my visiting aunt on her talented cooking. "Nonsense," my aunt replied, pointedly looking at me. "If you can read, you can cook!" I was impressed. Indeed, the ability to read and read well opens the world to us. If you can read, you can learn most anything. Reading is not a subject or skill that exists in isolation. The current emphasis on studying subjects "across the curriculum" recognizes this inter-dependency. The grammar that a student learns in Spanish class will help him understand English sentence structure. The logic that he learns in math class helps him to argue well with better organization on essay exams. The experimental techniques and scientific methods he learns in chemistry help him to both read and write more efficiently.

▲ *A Word to Parents*

As in other pursuits, there are fads in child development theories. Reading is the object of many such fads. For instance, as I write this book, TV ads hawk a correspondence reading program and a learning center course to improve reading. Yet, there are a few basic principles upon which to build reading. 1. Parents, themselves, should read. (See HABIT.) 2. The readiness factor has been proven; a child will read when he or she is "ripe" to read, when his internal clock says: "Now. Now, I am ready to make the leap-- to learn to read." 3. HOWEVER, parents must provide the rich environment *to allow* this to happen. A child kept in a walker will never learn to walk unaided. (See Pre-School thoughts throughout this book.) 4. Readiness also means that there will be a range of reading skills throughout elementary school. Consider this, but keep an eye out for problems. Laid back teens who are not avid readers need strong encouragement and serious discussion about their reading habits.

Serious reading problems are just as serious as any crippling health problem that can limit a child's potential. Get help, and if that source doesn't work for your child, try another source, and another, if necessary. Reading is a main key to the Kingdom of Knowledge and Understanding. In the Kingdom of Knowledge and Understanding is Wisdom. Through reading well, we can stand on the shoulders of the intellectual giants who have preceded us.

▲ *A Word to Teens*

If you are a good reader, get a reading list from a teacher or library: The books a good university recommends, a Great Books Foundation list, Harvard classics, etc. Read with college in mind, and read widely. (See DEPTH and BREADTH.) Reading widely means not only different authors and different periods, but also different genres: poetry, drama, journalistic work, humor, etc. One of my very favorite ploys is to get young people to choose to put away cheap pornography and replace it (if they are mature enough) with good, many times erotic, literature. Suggestion: *Siddhartha* by Hesse, Keats' "The Eve of St. Agnes," and as a challenge, James Joyce's *Ulysses*.

If you are a poor reader, capitalize on reading skills courses offered in high school; nothing is more important academically than being a good reader. There are many classic books with important content that are easy to read. Start with these. Ask your librarian for high level interest reads. You should aim toward understanding news magazines (*Time, Newsweek, U. S. News & World Report*, etc.) at a minimum. A good self-test of reading skill is whether you can readily understand the weekly essay on the last page of *Time* magazine. If you can, you have good reading skills. All good bookstores carry paperbacks on reading. You owe it to yourself to read. Commit: Start now.

▲ *A Word to Middle Schoolers*

You are a reader, whether or not you consider yourself a good reader! Keep reading in your life every day. Read many different types of things. For instance, you may be reading a how-to-make-paper airplanes book, the story of Martin Luther King, a Fear Street horror book, and a book of silly poems. On each birthday and Christmas list ask for, among all your wishes, a book or two. The ability to read means you have both knowledge (You *know* things.) and skills (You are able to *do* things.).   Knowledge needed includes such things as vocabulary, grammar, and sentence structure. Understanding these and recognizing what is logical helps you to analyze what you read, which is a critical skill. Challenge yourself by reading a book that is a little difficult.

▲ *A Word to Young Students*

Elementary students can ask for big books! Sometimes it's fun to carry around a huge, heavy book--feeling it reminds you reading is important. Some of these books are collections, like *Grimm's Fairy Tales*, and you can read them easily, a story or chapter at a time. Books you might ask to buy are intermediate dictionaries and word books. You do not have to understand every word in a book to enjoy it! Try some beautiful picture books. Not all picture books are for babies!

▲ *Pre-School thought*

My personal experience goes along with research that shows that children should be allowed to read before first grade. If the home environment is rich in materials and activities, and the parents have built good language skills through talking with and reading to their child, if language games are routine in play, then the child will probably learn to read before school. Certainly the current wonderful books and quality children's TV (Although I condemn most TV) are great boosts to reading. However, some children, even with a rich environment will not be ready. Further, when American education says: First grade = Learn to read, a few children will still not be ready. Don't worry. Unless your child is dyslexic or has other inhibiting problems, the youngster *will* read. If the child doesn't read efficiently in a year or so, certainly seek help from professionals. Even many adults have reading problems and deal with them effectively. Great progress has been made in the teaching of reading.

Red Hot Tips

☞ Students sometimes feel lost when reading and studying textbooks. The feeling is discouraging. Consider that the difficulty may not be your fault. Some textbooks are poorly written! (See TEXTBOOKS.) Take a breath, re-group (Walk around the room or do a few jumping jacks!), and approach the material with an attitude: You *can* read, and the material is a puzzle to be taken apart and solved.

☞ Prose that is truly easy to read is the hardest to write. Remember this when writing. Is it easy to read? Is your meaning clear?

☞ If there are passages in your assigned reading that are difficult, speak up. Ask your teacher to go over the material in her own words.

THESIS in (W)riting

Communication is often so full of babble, gobbledegook, and muddy language that we must say to ourselves, "Oh, yeah, I think he means...." Exactly what he *does* mean is not clear. We have come to accept vague gibberish from politicians and salesmen; and sadly, unclear language has crept into all aspects of our lives, scholarship included. To love language is to use it well.

▲ *A Word to Parents*

It's probable that many parents successfully completed their educations writing good reports. However, the distinction between a report and an essay with a THESIS is important, not only to good writing, but to clear thinking, and to many other aspects of scholarship.

A report and an essay are totally different. On the one hand, a report has a subject (and contains information about that subject.). On the other hand, an essay has one main idea, the THESIS. You can think of the difference in simple grammatical terms: A report is the subject, whereas an essay is the subject and a predicate, an opinion expressed in a complete sentence. A thesis is always expressed in a declarative sentence. A report gathers and presents straight-forward information on a subject; an essay (which by definition must have a thesis) uses information and ideas to say something about the subject, it gives an insight, it makes a conclusion, it expresses a point of view.

As adults we know that reading reports can be utterly boring whereas reading a thoughtful editorial or essay can be a lively experience that awakens all sorts of thoughts. Keep an eye on your student's assignments and homework to be sure that they regularly require the higher levels of thinking skills, that they do more than simply marshal information in reports, that they require real essays that are organized and advanced by a *thesis*. If the work in all grades does not reflect such opportunities for thinking, take the matter up with the teacher. Even elementary age students should be asked opinions.

Most parents would do well to listen to their children more carefully. Sometimes parents can help their children clarify their thoughts by asking them to re-state what they are saying. When you say, "Now, just what is your main point?" you are asking the child to order his thoughts and sub-ordinate some to others. In writing, subordinate points support the main idea which is the THESIS.

▲ A Word to Teens

Ironically, the concept of THESIS is difficult to understand because it is so simple. Teens think that THESIS is a funny word and that THESIS must be complex. Not so! A THESIS is simply the main idea of a paper or speech. An essay, for instance, may have many important ideas; but, in a good essay, they will support the *one* main idea, the THESIS. In fact, an essay is nothing more than a THESIS (main idea) developed and supported through the patterns of writing and speaking, e. g. cause and effect, comparison and contrast, analogy, etc. Study a good textbook on exposition. Try to pick up an introductory college exposition textbook from a 101 level class. Many are excellent.

▲ A Word to Middle Schoolers

When you are given a non-fiction writing assignment (not a story or poem), find out if the teacher wants a "report" or a paper with a main idea that is your opinion (THESIS) . A report would tell "All about dogs." An essay with a thesis about dogs might have, as the main point (or thesis), the opinion that "Dogs depend on humans more than cats do."

▲ *A Word to Young Students*

Making up stories about animals, cats, for instance, is creative writing.   Such stories might have titles like "Black Cat's Halloween" or "Kitten Gets A Surprise."   Think how you could make up a story to fit these titles.   Besides stories, you can also write what you think about something. What you think is called your "opinion."   Write down an opinion about cats, and then give examples.   Here is how this works.   Opinion: "Cats do tricky things."   Examples: "They tease dogs. They get into mother's yarn.   They hide in good places."

▲ *Pre-School Thought*

To help language skills develop, parents should be aware of using the four kinds of sentences: Interrogative (Questions). Exclamatory   (Exclamations).   Imperative   (Commands). Declarative (Statements).   Try   to   use   complete   sentences. Mixing the sentence types might confuse pre-schoolers.   "Put your shoes on; don't you want to do that?" sends two messages at once. This is one too many for a toddler. There is a need for all types of sentences as the child's language develops, but use the type which best fits your meaning. "Do you want your shoes on?" is much different from "We are going to put on your shoes."

Red Hot Tips

☞   In exposition (writing essays) the main point or THESIS is exposed. ("Expose" is derived from Latin, meaning to "set out".) The writer develops the THESIS/main idea, whether in a three page essay or a test answer in history class, states his

THESIS and sticks to it. Essays should not start with taxes and end with comments on drugs. A good THESIS will give birth to an OUTLINE, and the OUTLINE is your plan for the paper. Each part of the outline relates somehow to the main idea or THESIS.

☞ Part of your warm-up to write an essay or opinion paper should be to fold an index card and make a desk sign with your THESIS on it. Your THESIS should be one declarative sentence. With your THESIS in front of you, you will read/research and write toward your goal, and you will be aware of straying off your subject/THESIS. (See PREPARATION.)

☞ If there is the slightest confusion upon receiving a writing assignment, ask the teacher if he wants "a report," or "an essay with a thesis." You might even get your teacher re-thinking his assignment!

An important end note to parents and teens: While reports are necessary at times, writing essays is much more valuable to the student as a skill. Consider how HIGHER LEVEL THINKING SKILLS are involved. Writing reports develops clerical skills. The task requires gathering, sorting, and reporting the information, possibly through classification. It does not, in the main, involve any of the higher levels of thinking such as Analysis, Synthesis, and Evaluation (See Appendix A.). Traditionally students are first taught to write reports: "What I Did on Summer Vacation" or "All about Grizzly Bears." Woefully, many students are never asked, or even given the chance, to *think* about these subjects. Acquiring and disgorging information is enough to fulfill the requirements of many curricula and teachers. Is it any surprise that students find certain classes deadly dull?

TRANSITIONS

Internship helps make the change from medical student to practicing physician; newcomers' clubs help ease folks into new neighborhoods; the out-going officers meet with the in-coming. Transitions all! Transitions are important in life, and they are important in all good writing, whether in scholarship, business, or affairs of the heart.

▲ *A Word to Parents*

Sometimes parents are intimidated by the huge amount of educational jargon being thrown around. Most of the important-sounding terms are simply terms for sensible ideas. "Transition" is one such word. Check your teen's writing textbooks or a library for material on transitions. Also, read on.

▲ *A Word to Teens*

Transitions are devices which smooth writing. They are the bridges between ideas, especially between paragraphs. They can be words or phrases, e.g. "but," "then," "nevertheless," "on the other hand." Transitions can also be made repeating key words. End of paragraph 1: "I like baseball, but love *hockey*!" Start of paragraph 2: "*Hockey* has always...." Sometimes transitions are invisible, but they are there through logic: Consider three paragraphs: Mother, father, sister. What would the fourth be? Brother, of course. (Appendix B lists transitional words.)

▲ *A Word to Middle Schoolers*

Make a list of transitional words in your writing notebook or language skills notebook. These are words which signal what you are going to do next. Are you going to give an example? Then start the sentence: "For example...." Are you going to make an exception? Start: "However...." Sometimes there are many words for one meaning. For example, "and," "plus," "further," and "in addition" all mean that you are adding something to what you've said. (See appendix B).

▲ *A Word to Young Students*

Some words are like traffic signs. They are signal words. Examples of words that mean "stop" or perhaps "go in another direction" are "but" and "however." Words that mean go ahead are "also" and "plus." Use some of these signal words when you write.

▲ *Pre-School thought*

One of my earliest memories is being snatched from one activity and plunked into another. Even if you feel the language is beyond baby's understanding, voice the transition: "Let's leave the sandbox now, Sydney, and get washed up for dinner. We have watermelon!" or "Let's get dry and into your pajamas!" The child understands more than you think just from your tone.

RED HOT TIPS

☞ Vary your transitions in both position and type. You may put transitions at the end of a paragraph or at the start of the next. Transitional words will even appear in paragraphs between sentences.

☞ Use transitions carefully during exams and quizzes. Watch how they clarify your answers!

☞ Always proofread your work for transitions.

☞ Try using transitions in your speech, too. You'll be amazed at how they improve communication!

The Cutting Edge

GIFTED EDUCATION

"Gifted," a word that seems magical to mere ordinary mortals, is a problem to educators whose job is to define giftedness, set guidelines, and evaluate fair programs and budgets. The bottom line: Like scores, grades, and other evaluations, "gifted" isn't anything but a label. However, there are some generally accepted areas of giftedness. They are intelligence, creativity, task-commitment, leadership, and athleticism. First cousin to gifted is "talented," an exceptional, natural ability in art or music, too.

▲ *A Word to Parents*

Certainly some people are brighter than others, and some even seem to be the brightest around.   Further, some children will be ahead of the group, and viewed as *gifted* or *talented*, sometimes both!   These children need special attention, not only from teachers, but also from parents. Surprisingly, raising a gifted child is not an easy task. It is a demanding one, and parents will benefit from seeking professional guidance from school counselors (private psychologists, if necessary) and the excellent books on parenting gifted children available at any good library.   There are also several state and national organizations for information and support. (See below.) Parenting a child who might be brighter than the parent is a challenge, and the parent should constantly reassure himself that he is in charge, his instincts are good, and that he is providing the authority, love, and security that the gifted child, like all others, needs.

▲ A Word to Teens

The more highly gifted a teen is, the more alienated he or she might feel. A pediatrician once described being highly intelligent as "being in a room full of three year olds." Understanding that feelings of being different are normal for very bright kids helps gifted students cope with their differences. Intelligent and sensitive people perceive the world more intensely. Of course, they see the bad along with the good, and sometimes are troubled by their inability and powerlessness to right wrong. Further, giftedness does not mean maturity or omnipotence or even self-control. Gifted students should seek the support they need and deserve from knowledgeable adults. They should remember that they are not expected to be perfect. The gifted person is a human being first. Because of these special pressures, depression is common among gifted teen-agers, and they should ask for help. *On Being Gifted* (available through groups listed at the end of this chapter), a book written by gifted teens, themselves, is recommended reading. (See DEPTH & BREADTH.)

▲ A Word to Middle Schoolers

Middle Schoolers grow up in many directions and at many different speeds. Look around your class and note the different kinds of people! You'll probably find that many of your classmates have many different talents. What are yours? Are you so good at a subject that you are sometimes bored? If so, you might want to ask for further assignments. Sometimes you can dig deeper into a subject, do extra projects which are different from the class's work. If work seems "too stupid and boring" to do, talk to your teacher and to your parents. They will have some good ideas. (See DEPTH and BREADTH.)

▲ A Word to Young Students

Sometimes we're just like animals! My dog smiles (Yes,

he does!) when I say, "Good Red Rover!" When we are praised with "Good job!" or "Gee, are you smart!" we smile and feel good, too. But remember that words are just labels. When someone is called talented or smart, those words are just names for ideas the speaker has. We are all smart and talented in some ways!

▲ *Pre-School Thought*
Child-care books contain development guides; and of course, you can compare your toddler with others his age. Keep a patient eye on development, remembering that experts say there is a great latitude in the rate of development of pre-schoolers. One child will walk at nine months, another at 14; yet both are normal. One highly gifted toddler was a late talker. However, her first "word" was, "Give me a nickel." Keep your child's learning environment rich and safe. (See CREATIVITY.) If you see signs of very rapid development, start reading about giftedness. Encourage the widest range of suitable activities possible. A truly gifted child will lead the way if the learning environment is good.

Red Hot Tips
☞ Highly intelligent students may or may not be task-committed (have stick-to-itiveness). You all know really bright kids who are goof-offs with D averages. Try to strike a balance of work and play. Again, don't become obsessed with perfection.

☞ An excellent student might want to know all the answers. A highly gifted student may want to be sure that she does not miss any avenue of exploration. Think it over. In one way, answers are limits, and exploration is fun.

☞ Read widely. The following are especially recommended: J. D. Salinger's *The Catcher in the Rye, Nine Stories, Seymour: An Introduction,* and *Frannie and Zooey;* and Bradford's *Red Sky at Morning.*

☞ There are many excellent films (videos), some foreign, which give insight into intelligent and sensitive young people. Among them are *Little Man Tate, My Life as a Dog,* and *Prancer.*

☞ Highly intelligent and creative children often enjoy and benefit from the company of adults. Seek out adults that interest you in school, family circles, and neighborhoods and make adult "friends."

Where to write concerning giftedness:

American Association for Gifted Children
P. O. Box 2745
Dayton, OH 45401

The Association for the Gifted (CEC/TAG)
Council for Exceptional Children
1930 Association Drive
Reston, VA 22091
(Membership includes subscription to the quarterly, *Journal for the Education of the Gifted.*)

Office of Gifted & Talented Education, Dept. of Education
400 6th Street S. W. Room 3835
Washington, DC 20202

National Association for Gifted Children (NAGC)
NAGC   1155 15th Street   NW   Suite 1002
Washington, DC 20005
(Membership includes subscription to *Gifted Child Quarterly*.)

Supporting Emotional Needs of the Gifted (SENG)
School of Psychology
Wright State University
P. O. Box 2745
Dayton, OH   45401

Periodicals:
The Gifted Child Today
P. O. Box 637
Holmes, PA 19043

Gifted Child Quarterly
National Association for Gifted Children
1155 15th Street NW Suite 1002
Washington, DC 20005

National Research Center on the Gifted & Talented
University of Connecticut
362 Fairfield Rd., U-7
Storrs, CT 06269-2007

Journal for the Education of the Gifted
The University of North Carolina Press
P. O. Box 2288
Chapel Hill, NC 27515-2288

Journal of Secondary Gifted Education
P. O. Box 8813
Waco, TX 76714-8813

Our Gifted Children
Royal Fireworks Printing Company
First Avenue
Unionville, NY 10988

Roeper Review
Roeper City and Country School
P. O. Box 329
Bloomfield Hills, MI 48303-0329

Understanding Our Gifted
P. O. Box 18268
Boulder, CO 80308-8268

LEADERSHIP

"All kings," wrote Mark Twain in *Huckleberry Finn*, "is mostly rapscallions." This endearing line, like the other truths in Twain give his work a timelessness, along with its power and charm. And truth eternal the rapscallion line is, for today as then leaders and rascals have much in common: intelligence, creativity, flexibility, the social courage sometimes called "moxie" and that political nerve sometimes called "chutzpah."

▲ *A Word to Parents*
Teachers know less about the mechanics of leadership and what talents and abilities make a successful student leader than about most other aspects of education. What they *do* know, as Twain did, is that leaders take risks. Certainly, all dangers and consequences must be considered in risk-taking, and some risks are foolish. Nevertheless, strong leaders take risks, especially risks with probable successful outcomes. Remember this when your child seems to be rebelling or swimming against the popular current. He might be showing signs of leadership.

▲ *A Word to Teens*
I am sure you are sick of the word "conformity" and the phrase "peer pressure." Forget them. Follow your own instincts. Read old Ralph Waldo Emerson's famous essay, *Self-Reliance*. You're a good person, so you can follow your own right instincts. Keep a positive attitude (See SELF-ESTEEM.) and relax. Your conscience will kick in when you need it. At risk of having this book banned from your school library, I suggest that, when possible, you adopt the motto of most talented student leaders: "*It is easier to get forgiveness than*

permission." That's how the last sentence got into this book! (Review LISTENING as a leadership skill.)

▲ *A Word to Middle Schoolers*

A very important leadership quality is the ability to be a good listener. When you are working in a group or have been appointed captain, always listen to you classmates carefully. You can do this by 1. Giving them time to finish. 2. Giving everyone a chance to speak. 3. Repeating their feelings back to them, saying, "I understand that you feel..." Example: "that the science fair should be judged by rooms." Then say, "But I feel that it should be judged by grades." Have the courage to speak your opinions; if you do so calmly and nicely people will listen and respect your ideas.

▲ *A Word to Young Students*

Speak up! If you are a quiet person, even shy, practice speaking up by first writing down what you want to say. When the time comes, read it! For fun, you might like to use a special word. For example, write down, "Ms. Teacher, I liked that book *tremendously*." Then read the card to her! Read slowly. This also works when talking on the phone. Try it with grandparents.

▲ *Pre-School Thought*

Keeping simple tricks in mind during routine periods of play fosters leadership early on. One trick is encouraging the child to try new things or start the activity. The parent might say, "Now you go first!" Praise clearly and honestly when the child shows positive out-going behavior and safe risk-taking. The mastery of physical skills gives confidence. Naturally, safety always comes first for pre-schoolers!

Red Hot Tips

☞ Prepare for meetings by studying the issues to be discussed. Analyze issues and brainstorm solutions to problems.   Take notes just as you would while doing homework.   This preparation will save you time and also shorten the meeting. It is also a habit of good leaders.

☞   One educational model *(Renzulli)* talks about student potential in terms of intelligence, creativity, and task commitment. Add concern for others, desire for progress, and risk-taking, and you have a leader.

☞ Leaders need to be good speakers. Improve speaking skills by reading out loud and working hard on speeches for class. Teens can take such courses as debate, forensics, speech, and theatre arts. Tip within a tip: Most kids talk too fast when they speak formally in the classroom or at meetings.

☞ Teens who go to important meetings like leadership forums or student council meetings are not always forceful speakers. These young leaders should write their ideas out before a meeting, and early in the meeting offer their suggestions. They should put their paper on the table, clearly visible in front of them. The might of the pen and the power of print have been proven throughout history. Try this, you'll be astonished at the power of a written idea compared with a spoken idea. Adult leaders know that the first person to place a draft of a document on the table is most likely to have the greatest influence on the final decision.

PORTFOLIO

As Bob Dylan sang "For the times they are a-changin'." How true this is of *portfolio*, a fashionable term now in the Age of Information. Portfolio is confusing, however. It is frequently heard, but it is not always clear what is meant. This is because:

1. There are many kinds of portfolios for many diverse purposes, and 2. Often the speaker or writer, himself, is not always clear what he means. Generally a portfolio is some sort of repository for one's work and/or records.   Parents and students should study Appendix C, which not only explains how to make a student portfolio, but gives sample pages of actual students' work.

▲ *A Word to Parents*
Keep an eye on your children's portfolios to help them to make transitions from one stage of growth to another. Indeed, the teen's portfolio gives birth to the adult's resume. There are at least two things a parent can do. 1. Encourage the student to be aware of the concept of portfolio and make use of it in all possible projects. 2. See that he has a place to store portfolio items (not necessarily sort) and remind him to do so.

▲ *A Word to Teens*
You might ask teachers and counselors about portfolio. Your counselor's office will probably have some record of you in portfolio form, a folder of writing samples or interests at various ages. Such portfolios are mandatory in some states. Your writing teacher may ask you to keep your work and evaluation of it in a writing portfolio. You might ask for help to keep a record of your accomplishments, in and out of school,

to make a scholarship/college entry portfolio. Ask to see the portfolios of friends from other schools.

The purposes/uses/advantages of a personal high school portfolio are as an interview aid, an ice-breaker, a back-up system (You won't forget to mention a talent or honor!), a record-keeper, a means of showing your potential, accomplishment, and indiviudality.

▲ A Word to Middle Schoolers
Start a box for school things: sports, clubs, honors, and attendance certificates, programs from band concerts and plays. Save *all* papers on which the teacher marked "Good!" or "100%". Save things from outside of school, 4-H, church, and scouts. You do not need to glue things permanently in books. Keep them so you can *start* a portfolio when you *start* high school.

▲ A Word to Young Students
Keeping a scrapbook of school papers and mementos is fun! See if you can divide it into sections. How many ways can you divide it? By grade? By class? By art/crafts and reading and writing and math/science? Which do you think is the best way to divide it?

▲ Pre-school Thought
Parents should not stop record keeping with the baby book. When baby out-grows it, buy blank books to keep records current. As the child grows, look through the books with him or her.

RED HOT TIPS
☞ The more time and care you put into your portfolio, the more individual--different from all others--it will become.

The Higher Self

HONESTY

"I lost the book I stole from the library that I copied my paper from," my student said ingenuously. He smiled broadly about his accomplishment. He didn't realize his crime. Kids aren't bad, but often they do not *understand* what academic honesty *is* in these often careless, if not dishonest, times.

▲ *A Word to Parents*

Pressure on children for high grades, for steady and often rapid promotion, and ever-constant competition make optimum breeding ground for cheating. And cheating is exactly what copying, being half-truthful, and outright plagiarism are. Other words for it are only euphemisms and rationalizations. Ask the kids: "Everybody cheats!"

▲ *A Word to Teens*

"The biggest reason not to cheat is that *you will get caught.*" Students are always surprised when I say this rather than preach. However, it is true. Teachers have a 6th sense about dishonest work, and eventually cheats get caught. Think about cheating: Cutting corners (cheating), copying lab reports (cheating), giving answers to a pal (cheating), lying to the teacher about reading done (cheating), etc. It's a long list. Consider that cheating cheats the student. In the end, it erodes self-esteem; and worse, it destroys character. Advice: Find out about *unintentional* plagiarism (not giving proper credit for sources) and learn how to avoid it.

▲ *A Word to Middle Schoolers*

Some kids think that cheating is cool. It isn't. It's dumb and it's dangerous. Did you know that using someone's idea is cheating if you do not give him or her credit? Middle schoolers are old enough to take responsibility for their actions. Truthfulness and openness are always the best policy. If you didn't do your homework, admit it. Giving answers and letting friends copy is cheating, too. Even if you get a low grade because you don't know something and admit it, you will get an A for honesty and a "Good!" for character and citizenship. Good student leaders stick up for honesty.

▲ *A Word to Young Students*

If something is too hard, ask your teacher for help. If you do not know the answer, guess. If you are wrong, you still have done your best. Your wrong answer might be funny! It might even make you think of the right answer! Don't copy answers from friends. They may be wrong, and you would be a cheat *and you would know that.*

▲ *Pre-School Thought*

Check child development books on the use of words like "true," "real," and "story" at the age of your child. Be consistent, but not nagging, in your treatment of what is imaginary (and normal and healthy) and when you can and should make a distinction between reality and the imaginary. Lying in young children is a normal phase. Punishment has no place when the pre-schooler lies; the parent should simply say, "That is not true. People in our family tell the truth." Don't overreact.

RED HOT TIPS

☞ Teens should buy a good style sheet, *MLA* (Modern Language Association) or Kate Turabian's *Student's Guide for Writing College Papers*. They are very helpful in high school and nearly mandatory in college. Learn the proper way to give your sources credit.

☞ ALWAYS take notes in your own words, whether from the teacher's remarks or from your reading. This is a guard against unintentional plagiarism; and it is a way to process (study) the material. This becomes easier with practice. Use your own words. However, if you need key terms or vocabulary or exact axioms, copy them *exactly and note the source.*

QUIET

In his romantic philosophical work, *Sartor Resartus*, Thomas Carlyle says that "Silence is the element in which great things fashion themselves."

▲ *A Word to Parents*

Think about your home after dinner. Noise? Radio? TV? Stereos from your home and the one next door? Dishwasher? Telephone? Children shouting from different rooms? Lawn mowers next door? Street traffic? We commit a sin of omission by not recognizing how noisy our world has become, and we commit an even greater one by not *planning quiet*, orchestrating quiet, demanding quiet for our minds, nervous systems, and souls. Work for a noise ordinance in your community.

▲ *A Word to Teens*

You're a teen-ager, you're up front, you're sometimes rebellious, and life is loud. In the great roar of your life with your bright clothes, intense slang, loud music, there is a desperate need for quiet. Schedule quiet time before activities. Others do. Some drama coaches have a quiet night for the cast before opening night. Some athletic coaches use quiet time in locker rooms. If meditation and prayer require quiet, so do serious academic moments. Imagine a famous library at a great university-- Yale, Oxford, or Trinity College-- and you will imagine quiet.

▲ *A Word to Middle Schoolers*

Some families use "time out" to settle down rambunctious and excited youngsters. Older children, like you, can use time outs to be better students. Give yourself quiet times, even short ones of 10 minutes, in your room, on a walk, on the porch swing, and you will give yourself thinking time. Thinking time often means that you relax and get new ideas and remember things you know deep inside but were too busy to consider. Put your head down in school for a minute or two. Think about quiet before you go to sleep at night and you will sleep well.

▲ *A Word to Young Children*

When noise and confusion bother you in school, make a list of good things that happen quietly. You might start it like this: Clouds move, plants grow, fish swim. Spend a few minutes thinking of quiet things, then start your work again.

▲ *Pre-School Thought*

Every household, every child, every baby needs some quiet time. Veterinarians suggest that even animals need periods of quiet for well being. Let your youngest children enjoy the serenity of quiet along with the energies of talk, music, and life's pleasant sounds.

RED HOT TIPS

☞ If you feel you *must* have music to study to, you need to practice quiet. Start quiet with small periods of time and work up to at least one hour. There will be times in school and other places where you will have to do your best work without music. Walkmans are not allowed during ACT or SAT testing. You will never see a bride, a groom, a goalie, or a newborn with a Walkman.

☞ You surround a fine work of art with a frame, a great photograph with a mat, the important points in your notes with space on the page. Think of quiet space around you when you work or take a test. Fill it with positive thoughts: intelligence, creativity, knowledge.

☞ Try doing homework to Mozart, even if you are not a classical music fan.

SELF-ESTEEM

"I celebrate myself, and sing myself...." When I teach Walt Whitman's *Song of Myself*, I first ask students to stand and raise their arms joyfully. Second, I ask them what types of things mankind celebrates; and third, to brainstorm what man sings: love ballads, drinking songs, rap, funeral hymns, and more. How wonderful is the miracle of man! And, being human, why shouldn't we love and respect ourselves as well as others? If we do not honestly love and respect ourselves, how can we honestly thank God or creation for our lives.

▲ *A Word to Parents*

Many educational "breakthroughs" turn out to be passing fads in the end. However, the current emphasis in American education on self-esteem is an exception. In very simple terms, whether the vocabulary is from Freud or *from Transactional Analysis*, the healthy psyche includes the super-ego (*parent*), the id (*child*), and importantly--the ego(*adult*). As a healthy man has a healthy appreciation of himself, the fit student has respect for his mind, its processes, its ideas, and its products.

▲ *A Word to Teens*

Develop a cheerleading program for yourself, your physical appearance, your emotional system, your mind, your past, present, and future. Appreciate your individuality. Trials, doubts, emotional swings, and confusion are ever-present during the teen years. That's normal! Scour the landscape of your life for good things about you! Make a portfolio (See PORTFOLIO.) Keep a "good news" diary. List achievements! Avoid critical people, gossips, and doom-sayers. Practice self-esteem on the small details. Proclaim yourself as Whitman does, and live deliberately as Thoreau sought to do. Badges, buttons, and T-shirts can help you assert your best convictions. Let your actions bespeak your best thoughts. Join the intellectual, political, or religious community: Become an informed citizen. Write to your congressman and your newspaper editor. Enjoy your kinships with the natural world: Keep living things (plants, fish, and other pets) around you, and don't feel silly about talking to them. Give them funky or up-beat names. Nurturing is good. (See ATTITUDE.)

▲ *A Word to Middle Schoolers*

Sometimes we think we are too fat or too thin, too tall or too short. Sometimes we think we are ugly because we wear glasses or braces or have a wart. At these times, remember that how someone "looks" is not what someone "is." Keep a special bulletin board in you room for things you especially like, nice notes from friends and parents, postcards with good lookin' animals, and good work you have done. Make a list of 10 famous people, then find their pictures in the library. Try Abraham Lincoln, Eleanor Roosevelt, Orson Wells, and Albert Einstein. Now look in the mirror and smile.

▲ *A Word To Young Students*

Start a collection of something you like, perhaps something no one else has! Leaves? Caps? Postcards from different states? Make a poster of your name in different designs. Draw a pie cut into pieces, and label each piece with one of your talents.

▲ *Pre-School Thought*

A toddler cannot receive enough praise! However, honesty, timing, and appropriateness of the praise are critical. The parent might engage in active-listening (repeating the child's words back to him) at praiseworthy times, e. g. "You think your hands are very strong? Oh, I do, too!" Hugs are good. Physical touching raises self-esteem. When the child has had enough, he or she will wander off to play.

Red Hot Tips

☞ Show your stuff! If you are good in art incorporate art, in every possible way, in your work--draw sketches in test answers, suggest art projects for class. If you are orderly, use order in your work--make charts and lists, suggest how to set up class projects. Ride every horse in the stable, but race with your strongest horses.

☞ No matter how ugly the incident, how poor the job, how low the grade, remember and emphasize, the situation is only the incident, the particular job, or the one grade. It is not *you*, not the person, the student, the soul. You are worthy of appreciation and respect. As a character named Scarlet O'Hara said, "Tomorrow is another day."

☞ The best selling psychotherapist, M. Scott Peck, believes that healthy self-esteem and self-awareness lead not only to important virtues, but to civility itself. (See BEHAVIOR.)

SERVICE/ALTRUISM

"It is more blessed to give than to receive." Never has this been truer than for today's students.   For today, "giving," "stewardship," and "service" are magic words.   In a world society where selfishness and greed seem prevalent, the youth who believes in "giving" is truly blessed, not only with a strong and healthy sense of community, but also with the way his teachers view him as well as how he appears on a college application.

▲ *A Word to Parents*
Some high schools now require a certain number of community service hours as a requirement for a diploma. Most high school honor societies require individual or group community or charitable work. An art club paints the town ice-skating shed with amusing murals; the academic honor society sponsors the blood drive; the journalism honorary tends a memorial garden. Parents can also encourage service in their children.   Beside the all-important parental example, simple ways to do this are pointing out opportunities for the student to help others, allowing means and time for such help, and praising children for selflessness.

▲ *A Word to Teens*
We live in an age where there is much discussion about roles in society: the individual, family, political party or business. What works? What's right? In spite of all this confusion, there is a philosophy than can and does work today as it always has: *Altruism*, the unselfish concern for others. It's easy because it starts with a kind, generous attitude about the little things. It is important to students since today's adult leaders look for youth

who care about their world and the people in it, young people who are willing to give both their time and talents to aid humanity. These are the teens who will succeed, who will get into the choice universities, and who will win the scholarships. "I want to be an engineer so I can be rich," never got a student into a college.

▲ A Word to Middle Schoolers

Having a favorite color, a favorite author, and a favorite music group is fun. Having a favorite charity is more than fun. It makes you feel good about yourself! Ask if you can join a walk for hunger! Go through your clothing and ask if you can re-cycle old things to charity. Collect pop cans and turn in the refunds to the humane society! Make a list of charities, and pick one you want to work for!

▲ A Word to Young Students

Helping other people is strange. You usually end up feeling very good, as if someone helped you! Pick a different person each day to help! "What can I do to help you?" Ask your teacher on Monday, your mom on Tuesday, your father on Wednesday, and so on. Also, help immediately, if you can, whenever you see a chance to do so! Helping others also makes life interesting. The next time you have "nothing to do," help someone. You can even send a cheery picture to your grandparents or make pictures to send to children in hospitals. Ask your teacher if your class can do this.   ·

▲ Pre-School Thought

Children, before two, still need mother, and mother is all to them. They will not benefit from encouragement to share, to think of others. You may serve as role model, and your doing so may satisfy you, but do not expect concern for others to start until the child is ready. He may engage in parallel play with other toddlers, but he probably won't interact. Again, readiness is an individual matter. At about two, however, the child can start to help mother, handing her things in the kitchen, mopping up a spill, etc.   Then, miracles happen at three: A child's anxieties lessen, and he will begin interaction in play this year, begin to share, and develop his concern for other human beings. He is on his way.

RED HOT TIPS

☞ Develop a list of words, including synonyms, for "love." Greek is a rich language, and there are many Greek words for our simple word, "love." Look up the Greek word, "agape." Remember it when you experience the feeling of helping others.

☞ First think of the ways you have been of service to others. Write them down. Now, build on that list through actions, and mention the word "service" on all applications when you can.

Appendix A

Thinking Skills

Educational jargon and the associations of some words often cause students and parents to be wary of higher level thinking skills. "Higher level" brings visions of magic crystals, tricks of meditation, or pyramid power to some. Words like "taxonomy" sound complicated and suspicious.

I would like to dismiss this distrust here and now: "Higher Level Thinking Skills" are simply the most efficient ways of thinking, thinking when our brains are working very well. People using their brains analyzing, synthesizing, or evaluating are like people driving a well engineered, finely tuned car.

Most higher level thinking charts in books and on posters in classrooms are based on the work of Benjamin Bloom, an educator who worked at the University of Chicago. He developed a "taxonomy"--a classification of the many ways students, teachers, and all people can think about a great variety of subjects. Thus, the term "Bloom's Taxonomy" is the term often used when discussing or using Higher Level Thinking Skills.

Good teachers understand the system, and make use of the Higher Level Skills (analysis, synthesis, and evaluation) in their work. I like to take the advantage one step further and teach the system to students, themselves, thereby arming them with a strong academic tool for use any time, any place, in any of their education or work.

The following explains the six levels of thinking in Bloom's taxonomy, Knowledge being the most basic. The complexity of thought increases at each level and culminates in Evaluation.

KNOWLEDGE

Knowledge is remembering. It is a toddler saying, "1-2-3! 1-2-3!" when he does not yet understand counting. *Knowledge* is recalling and recognizing: "That's a mule," but not knowing exactly what a mule is.

Words used at this level include: cluster, circle, copy down, define, label, list, match, memorize, name, recall, underline, etc.

COMPREHENSION

Comprehension is understanding. The child can count three objects. He can explain what a mule is and find a mule in an animal book.

Words used at this level include: cite, describe, find, review, show, summarize, understand, etc.

APPLICATION

Application is using your knowledge and understanding. The child can count pennies for a roll. The child draws a mule in a farm picture.

Words used at this level include: apply, choose, demonstrate, illustrate, imitate, model, select, use, etc.

ANALYSIS

Analysis is taking material or a problem apart. Much is learned and problems are solved by breaking down the whole into its parts. The student can make change for a dollar in different ways. He can analyze a mule by noting its diet, habitat, temperament, etc.

Words used at this level include analyze, break down, characterize, classify, compare, contrast, divide, examine, take apart, etc. The student should practice different kinds of analysis. Trucks, for instance, can be broken down by color, manufacturer, pulling capacity, etc.

SYNTHESIS

Synthesis is putting things back together in a new way, restructuring, adding things or deleting things. The student converts some of his money into bonds. He uses the mule as an attraction in a circus story.

Words used at this level are blend, change, construct, combine, compose, create, develop, formulate, invent, invert, propose, re-shape, speculate, suppose, what if, etc. Students should consciously use synthesis during creative activities and problem solving.

EVALUATION

Evaluation is the work of the philosopher king or a wise person. *Evaluation* means making judgments, arriving at considered opinions. The student evaluates the economy or reviews a play. The mule is assessed for his efficiency.

Words used at this level, often on essay tests, are argue, convince, criticize, debate, persuade, rank, recommend, etc.

Appendix B

Transitional Words: A Guide

Language is the great enabler of clear, discreet thought. A child cannot think additively without "and" and "also." Once these little words are in place, we hear almost endless strings of things and sequential events. Think of the birthday list.

"But" and "however" unleash a torrent of pent-up contrariness and exceptions. The words make the thought processes capable of expression and encourage tons of comparisons, analyses, and evaluations. All this is great stuff for the growing brain since it apparently stimulates synapse formation much as physical exercise encourages sound muscular and skeletal growth. Thought enabling words may be as important to the brain as vitamins and minerals are to the whole body.

(Lists of some words to use regularly in writing)

Teen and Adult

Addition: also, and, and then, first (second, third, etc.), furthermore, moreover, not only...but also, plus, too, etc.

Comparison: in such a manner, likewise, similarly, etc.

Contrast: but, however, nevertheless, still, on the contrary, on the other hand, otherwise, yet, etc.

Place: beyond, here, nearby, there, opposite, etc.

Result: As a result, consequently, hence, so, therefore, thus, etc.

Time: afterward, after a while, before, finally, first , immediately, later, meanwhile, soon, then, last, etc.

To show various other relationships (to summarize, emphasize, to re-phrase, etc.) : For example , for instance, indeed, in fact, insofar as,   on the whole, re-stating, therefore, to exemplify

Middle Schoolers

and
but
however
nevertheless
then
yet

Young Students

also
and
but
then
yet

Pre-Schoolers

and
then
but

Teaching transitions in writing is usually fun for the teacher and the students. The idea of transitions, bridges in writing, is usually new to students and therefore fresh.   Using transitions in different places, experimenting with the different kinds, and evaluating their effects often fascinates students of writing. What an easy and effective tool!

I believe that we all would benefit from being more aware of transitions in our lives, too, alert to the ramifications of sudden or unexpected changes in routine or groups, whether family, social, business, or political. Indeed, we are smart to arm ourselves with "emergency kits" of stress busting techniques for these times. (See STRESS.)

Further, even the happiest of transitions, going to a challenging wilderness camp, moving into a new home, being promoted in grade school or in business, involve stress. How many comedies have been made about the stress of weddings?

My students have always been fascinated with the theme of initiation in literature, the transition (through pain and new knowledge) from one status to another. Telemachus, son of Odysseus, becomes a man. The halfback is thrown into the shower when he makes the varsity. Thinking about such rituals, readying ourselves for change and growth, is wise.

Transitions during a child's growth include new schools, new subjects, new teachers, hormonal change, moves, changes in family, birth of siblings, divorce, death of grandparents, and changing desires and needs..   Families need to be aware of transitions in life as the wise student is aware of transitions in his writing.

Appendix C

Personal Student Portfolio

Why are students using personal portfolios? Very simply put, they use portfolios to show their work to prospective clients, employers, or evaluation committees for grants or scholarships. A portfolio gives concrete evidence of abstract claims of talent, ability, expertise, and productivity.

So, in the same manner, in an interview with a college admissions officer, a student with a 3.5 GPA might respond to a direct question about his grades, "I have a 3.5." The officer knows that a 3.5 is a B+/A- average which is good, but not very memorable or remarkable--especially among the excellent students who apply to selective colleges.

But, if the student has his portfolio in his hand, he can open it to the transcript page and say, "I have a 3.5 GPA, and I've high-lighted all the honors, accelerated, and advanced placement courses I've taken. I'm especially proud of this A- in pre-calculus because the teacher is a very tough grader and has his master's degree from Einstein U."

The student can then turn to the School Profile page and point out that they are fortunate to have many teachers with advanced degrees, that they send a high percentage of students to college, or that the school ranks high on state proficiency tests, whatever the case may be. Or, he might show how he has supplemented his work at a modest rural school by reading widely and taking on interesting projects.

This is an example of both "Show, not tell!" and "Specific is terrific!" The student has made the quantum leap from being a mere cipher on a page to being a fully individuated, actual person. That is what a student's personal portfolio is all about: going from the abstract claim to the real blood, muscle, and brains person without moving from the interview chair--in some cases without even being there, as when he is being considered for a scholarship or admission by a committee half a continent away. Conveniently, portfolios can be mailed!

A student's personal portfolio differs considerably from the formal record portfolio which most schools now keep in the counselor's or principal's office. The school's portfolios are unedited records that usually accurately represent the student's work and school life as annual entries are recorded, but they do not allow the student to focus, to present himself or herself as a scholar-athlete, or as a creative, musical person, or as a budding diplomat who has an intense interest in international affairs, is taking a foreign language, and has applied for foreign exchange.

This personal focus is what gives the student's personal portfolio the keen edge. Properly constructed (with care and work), the student's portfolio should be an unabashed celebration of the student as a developing individual. It should not read like a technical evaluation, a straight news story or-- worse-- a family scrapbook.

Ideally, it should read like a human interest story, a success story of hard work, good attitudes, and potential. It should also reflect a happy kid. The reader should look for these reflections in the sample portfolio pages at the end of this appendix which were created by successful students.

The Uses and Advantages of the Personal Portfolio

The personal portfolio
... makes record keeping easier
... breaks the ice at interviews
... enriches interviews
... safeguards against "flubs" and omissions (Accomplishments you wish to emphasize are captured in your portfolio. You don't have to worry about forgetting to mention them.)
... represents you *in absentia*
... gives you an edge; or at the minimum keeps you up to date with current student practices
... builds self-esteem
... documents on-going growth
... allows you to explain or de-emphasize weaknesses
... can be used for summer jobs, career-oriented programs, college application supplements, and scholarship and award opportunities.

One clear advantage of personal portfolio use is that, as the student edits, he can control the way he is perceived. Further, the student "puts the ball into the interviewer's court" by placing his portfolio on the interviewer's desk. This is to say that the interviewer will react to items in the portfolio which naturally interest him. The student won't waste time talking about his poetry when the interviewer is most interested in his leadership skills.

A very practical advantage is that students can direct (or mail) portfolios to the person or department they judge to be friendliest, most interested, or helpful. A student musician, for instance, might gain extra support by sending his portfolio to the music department and asking for a recommendation.

I know of one infamous, local interviewer for an Ivy League school who started all interviews with the statement, "I want you to know that no one I've interviewed has ever been accepted." Surely, this man should be avoided and the portfolio sent to another representative.

The student will find that once he works with his portfolio, new ideas and uses will come to him!

Suggested Supplies for the Personal Portfolio

... Vinyl covered three-ring notebook in a business-like color although pink, orange, and turquoise work for artists and dancers.
Ring binders are necessary for easy access and rearrangement.
... Inexpensive page protectors. Buy a full box for later use.
... Stationery, assorted labels, assorted office supplies
... Double sticky-sided tape (This secures documents. Some glues react with the page protectors and shrink wrap your portfolio!)
... Index cards (if you wish to hand-write editing cards)
... Access to a laser printer and a photocopier (Many copy shops rent time for computers and printers if you cannot use your school's)

Guidelines for Organizing a Portfolio

General Principles:

A personal portfolio is a "living" thing.   The number of pages and sections grows as students gain experience and new interests.   Contents are re-arranged as the purpose changes: The order of pages would be different, for example, if a person were on the one hand applying for a job as a counselor at a summer camp or on the other hand presenting oneself as a candidate before a scholarship committee.

When you do have advance notice, always write an introductory letter to a specific addressee (Dear Dean McBrain or Dear Gold Star Committee Members), focused to the specific subject (admission to Podunk or The Gold Star Scholarship).

Never think of your portfolio as a mere scrapbook or you doom it to mediocrity.

Avoid chronological order.   Order should be a tool for emphasis.   While you do want to balance more formal items like records with more upbeat things like work samples, you also want to put your best foot, your desired foot, forward-- early in the portfolio.

Since the very first page is a letter in which you introduce yourself (*as you care to be perceived*), as a student-athlete or a service oriented student of government or a young scientist who is possibly a pre-medical student, the reader will expect to see materials that reflect this early in the portfolio.   So, the government student might have first pages that contain evidence of team leadership, or field trips to government centers, or of social studies fair entries.

The Opening Letter:

A word about the opening letter, the first page of the portfolio. A general "Letter to the Reader" should always be in the first page protector when your portfolio is not in use. This means your portfolio is "ready to go" should an opportunity suddenly arise. I know of one student who handed her portfolio over in an instant as a visiting insurance salesman told her father of the company's scholarship program. Her portfolio was ready, the salesman hand-carried it to the company, and she got a scholarship!

While order of materials is important, remember that the order of a portfolio is never set in cement. Ring binders make changing the orders of pages and sections easy. For a Law Association's scholarship, debate activity and English grades are moved forward; for a sporting goods scholarship, sports pages move to the front.

Showing personality and Indiviudality:

After you have focused on your main interest and strength, create a section which gives evidence of your personality. Show that you are an individual who is a quiet creator; or a lively, demonstrative school leader; or an original thinker, artist or musician. This section is also a chance for you to balance weaknesses or prevent misconceptions.

One student of mine, an orderly only child, had 4.0 GPA, and worked in school, house, community, and church. However, her carefully crafted portfolio could be described in one word: BORING. After some thought, we found an event that brought humanity (and some humor) to her life. When this student was the mature and wise age of 17, her mother did the unthinkable.   Her mother became pregnant and delivered a sibling to our student. How her life changed!   And, how her portfolio changed when the student included a section of witty detail and evidence of the experience of going from only child to the member of the chaotic household of a newborn.

One clever idea that has been successful with students is to "map" some aspect of their lives.   Such maps might represent sports philosophy, respect of family, hopes and goals, values, or even the student's thinking process.

Editing cards or notes

Editing cards or notes can be hand-written (A swell idea if you happen to have a distinctive hand!) or done by computer and printer.   On them the student comments, editorializing (giving slant and emphasis) on the page material.   He gives amplifying information, he interprets the importance of the page, and possibly evaluates the effects of the accomplishment.

When you write your editing cards, you have the chance to show your skill and perception.   Further, along with your discerning judgment, you can show very desirable traits such as appreciation and gratitude for others for their roles as teachers or role models. For instance, part of a card on drama might read, "I played Titania in the fall play, *A Midsummers Night's Dream*.   The director named me Best Actress.   Doing Shakespeare is rare for a small school, but we have nearly a professional director and a very active, talented group of thespians." This card shows intelligence, appreciation of others, skills at analysis, and also a good vocabulary.

skills at analysis, and also a good vocabulary.

Classy people are not snobs; they are gracious and humane. The portfolio is an excellent place to exhibit your class act.

Envelopes

At the end of your portfolio (inside the back cover), place two large manila envelopes. Mark one "Samples of Schoolwork" and in it enclose longer samples of good work. For instance, page 1 of a major term paper might be included earlier in the writing section of your portfolio. The editing card on that page would read, "This is a sample of my geometry paper on topology. The complete paper is in the Samples of Schoolwork envelope at the end of this portfolio." If the reader happens to be interested in reading the whole paper, he can, but the bulk of the paper is kept to the portfolio's end, in the sample envelope.

The second envelope should be self-addressed to you (neatly!) with enough postage to return it..

Sample Portfolio Pages from
a 10th Grade Class

The work on these pages was done by students in an
Honors English Class, Seminar in the Essay
Elk Rapids High School
Elk Rapids, Michigan

The following students contributed selected pages of their personal portfolios to serve as samples. The author thanks them.

Rex Graff III is a "Renaissance kid" in the sense of being athlete, scholar, journalist, thespian, leader, and good friend. He takes on a wealth of activities, and attacks each with full energies. He calls himself "determined," and he is willing to work to attain lofty goals. Besides being a top football player, playing the lead in the school plays, co-leading an area leadership Forum, he is also a winning debater. Rex thinks kids will succeed if they work hard, persevere, keep thinking and listening, and keep open minds.

David Ketchum, the author's youngest son, made one of the first portfolios in his school at the suggestion of a gifted education counselor. It was a factor in his college applications since he entered college early, at age 16. David has a degree in pure math from Northwestern University and now works in management in California. He enjoys people, animals, roller blades, good food, and good weather.

Jathan Manley went to the awards table many times at his senior class honors assembly. He won the departmental honors in Communication Arts, Math, and Science. An exceptionally talented computer scientist, he "serves" by helping other students, including the yearbook staff, and especially as production manager of the school paper. Seemingly able to do the work of many, he has also student directed the school play, and is a talented actor himself. He loves music and plays the trumpet. Yet Jay is quiet and humble, a serious thinker with a wry wit--a class act, indeed.

Samuel Tegel is a smart student with drive and focus. He is aware of his position as the oldest of four brothers; and, as his map shows, he respects "family." He believes in hard work, taking on responsibility, and service. He's active as an athlete (basketball and baseball), a debater, a student council member, and a member of Science Olympiad. He hopes to attend a highly selective univerisity and is currently open-minded about his field of study.

Philip Wells is a many-sided young man. He is a farm boy (the farm complete with a roadside farm market), an excellent student with an exciting interest in computer science, an athlete on both the golf and tennis teams, and a musician who plays a sweet trombone.   In his own words, he's fun-loving and outgoing; others find him kind and compassionate.   His philosophy is that if you find happiness in what you do, you'll find success.   Philip hopes to go to Michigan Technological University.

Nora Wiltse is a student   at Albion College.   She is an energetic, intelligent young woman of great integrity.   She is sincere and task-commited in her work and views the world very   thoughtfully.   She   is   an   accomplished   musician (percussion). Many high school activities, including journalism, prepared her for her active campus life.   She is in the Albion Student Senate, the Marching Band, and on the tennis team.

Tara Zeigler is a dancer. As a matter of fact, she is in motion most of the time whether dashing from a meeting to a play practice.   Tara is also a very talented actress who combines her grace from dance into subtle stage movements, tragic or comic. She is widely read, took AP litereature as a junior, and is a sophisticated lady in the best (and proper) sense of the word.

Ten emotions of the comical game we call Golf.

Many athletes like to map their personalities on sports territories. Note the various approaches.

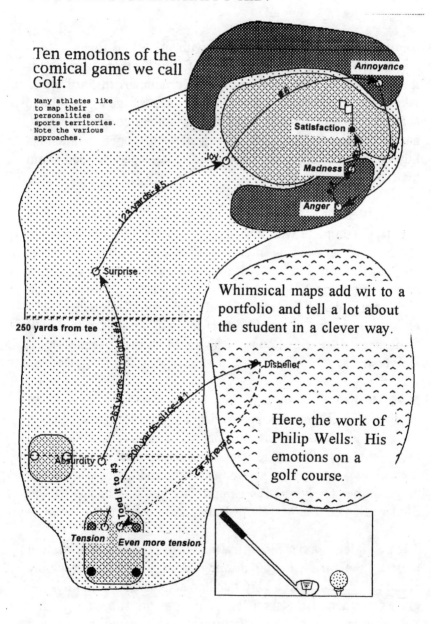

Annoyance

Satisfaction

Madness

Anger

Joy

#6

122 yards-#5

Surprise

250 yards from tee

263 yards-straight-#4

200 yards-slice-#1

Whimsical maps add wit to a portfolio and tell a lot about the student in a clever way.

Disbelief

Absurdity

Toed it to #3

Here, the work of Philip Wells: His emotions on a golf course.

Tension   Even more tension

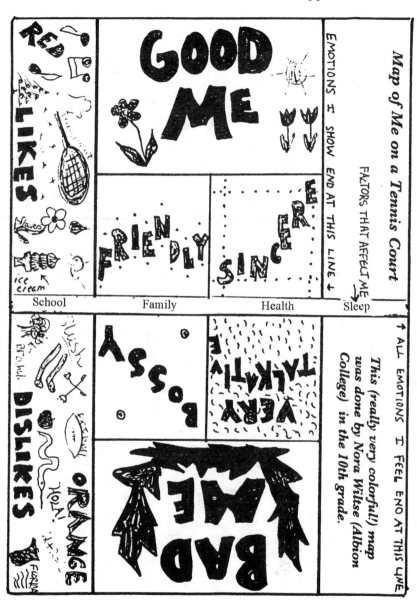

Map of Me on a Tennis Court

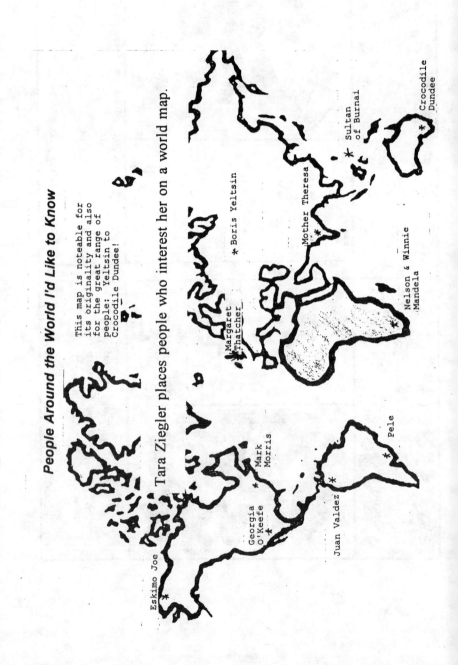

People Around the World I'd Like to Know

This map is noteable for its originality and also for the great range of people: Yeltsin to Crocodile Dundee!

Tara Ziegler places people who interest her on a world map.

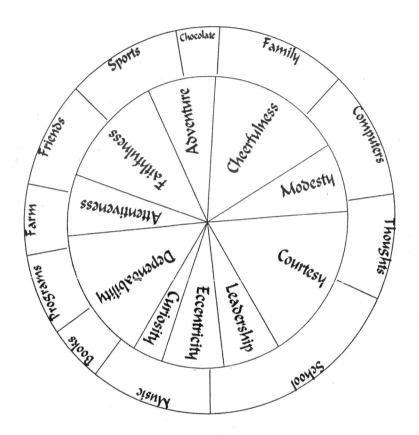

Philip Wells uses two pie charts to show how he applies his virtues to aspects of his life. Centered with an ordinary paper fastener in his portfolio, the reader easily imagines Philip's very full life, his talents in action.

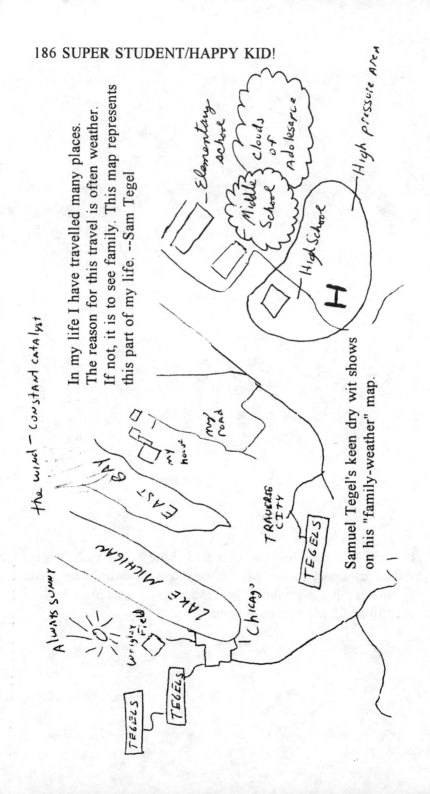

In my life I have travelled many places. The reason for this travel is often weather. If not, it is to see family. This map represents this part of my life. --Sam Tegel

Samuel Tegel's keen dry wit shows on his "family-weather" map.

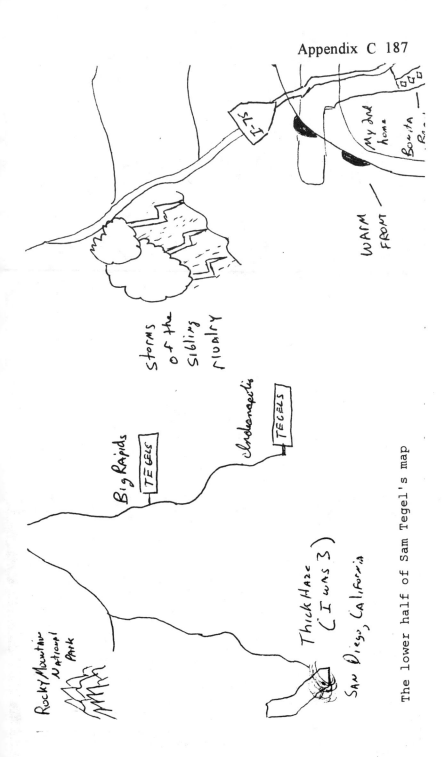

The lower half of Sam Tegel's map

Clippings from the school and town papers, along with an editing card, display Rex's success in drama.

"Father of the Bride" was my second ERHS drama involvement. With a larger role than the previous, I learned that it is an honor to contribute as a group the best of one's abilities for the cast, the performance, and ultimately - the audience.

Photo by Bill Gast

Opening the gifts

ther of the bride Stanley Banks (Bill Breznau) and mother Ellie Banks (Pam Adams), k on as prospective bride and groom, Kay Banks (Gretchen Gast) and Buckley nstan (Rex Graff), open one of the many wedding gifts in last week's Elk Rapids High hool Drama Club's production of Father of the Bride.

Wedding "Guests" loved it all: Bride a success
by April Maylone

Father of the Bride was this year's successful choice for the fall drama production. Starring Gretchen Gast, Bill Breznau, Rex Graff, and Pam Adams, the play was a heartfelt comedy, a warm story of the wonders and worries of a young woman being married while her father feels he is losing his baby.

Math teacher, Dave Parks, summed up the performance: "Congratulations to the cast and crew. The actors were convincing. Elly made me feel warm and loved. I saw my own grandfather in Stanley, Buckley made me laugh, and Kay stole my heart! The set was incredible, the lighting was profession, and the costumes were exquisite. A WONDERFUL performance, emmys for all!"

Jeff Powers, a.k.a. Siskel or Ebert, commented, "I give it two thumbs up. However, I would have taken the money and eloped."

All in all, thanks for a good job to all involved in the play, especially to director Lin Opgenorth and student director Wayne Geisert.

Science Olympiad has been a part of my spring since eigtl grade. As a freshman, I recieved a first place at regionals fo "Sounds of Music", where we make and play our ow: intruments; "Road Rally", where we read differnt kinds c maps; and "Simple Machine", in which you have to calculai the forces that work on simple macines.

Our whole team won first place at regionals, and we wen on to state. Here, a friend and I placed third in "Road Rally one of only two events from our team to place at state.

In my mind, Science Olympiad is a great way to lear competition and hard-working skills.

Philip Wells' creative representation of his participation in Science Olympiad: Photocopied medals.

MEMBERSHIP
HAS ITS
PRIVILEGES

Rex Graff III, a leader who is involved in most activities, uses a bit of ironic humor to show that, in spite of all his honors, he doesn't take himself *too* seriously.

Rex
Rex Graff
Elk Rapids High
Williamsburg, MI
& Communicati

National Honor Society
Membership Card

AWARD TO   Rex Graff III

ADVISER
Dale S. Hawley

SECRETARY, THIS NATIONAL COUNCIL
DIRECTOR, NASSP DIVISION OF
STUDENT ACTIVITIES

DIRECTOR, N.A.S.P.
THE NATIONAL ASSOCIATION OF
SECONDARY SCHOOL PRINCIPALS

Quill and Scroll

International Honorary Society for High School Journal

This is to Certify that *Rex Graff III*
of the *Elk Rapids* High
Chapter of Quill and Scroll, having satisfied the requirements of the organization and is entitled to the Rights, Benefits, and Honors which everywhere pertain there

NATIONAL ART HONOR SOCIETY
for High School Students

A Service of
The National Art Education Association

Name REX GRAFF

Signature Rex Graff

Chapter 905

CHAPTER MEMBERSHIP CARD

The International Thespian Socie
A component of the Educational Theatre Assoc

THIS CERTIFIES THAT

REX   GRAFF

FOR MERITORIOUS PARTICIPATION IN THEATRICAL
IS A MEMBER OF INTERNATIONAL THESPIAN SOC
TROUPE NUMBER

Theater & Dance

Artwork on a title page...

Tara Ziegler's interests and experiences merit a whole section on the performing arts. Here is her title page.

Certificate of Recognition to

Tara Zeigler ~ 2nd place

for participation in the
Van Gogh Self-Portrait
Contest sponsored by the
Traverse City Record-Eagle,
the Dennos Museum and
the Downtown Traverse
City Association.

This award certificate
is striking: Van Gogh
is on it. It was placed
prominently in the
portfolio.

Tara Ziegler

You might see me in a bright, hot, stuffy studio dancing like a woman possessed. And if you looked closely enough, you would notice my eyes, burning emeralds showing my passion for dance and an endless need to be better. You would see them conveying my urge to push my body to its limits. You'd see then hold back tears of agony as I fall while doing a triple pirouette. You would see them glass over with determination as I get up to try again.

Behind my eyes, deep in my psyche, somewhere in that jumbled muddle of hopes, fears, and dreams, lies the purpose of my fascination with dance. Is it the artistry? I am bound only by my imagination to create impossible shapes, breathtaking positions, and abtruse lines. Movement set to music inspired from a choreographer's soul can move others.

Is it to pay homage to Martha Graham? Intricate workings of the hands? Becoming one with the floor? Is it applause? Praise? Or is it more than that? My choice. No choice. Dancing is my destiny.

Competitions are excellent portfolio material, whether or not you have won them. They show that you take the initiative and are willing to take risks!

Over 600 students enrolled in honors English classes from 29 schools in the area participated in the Van Gogh self-portrait contest. It was quite an honor to receive second place!

SEMESTER ENDING

```
30 960560 GRAFF REX III              M09- 3530 960560 GRAFF REX III          M09
22MUN ALGEBRA I          A- 0.50        822MUN ALGEBRA I              B  0.50
43HOC DEBATE             A  0.50     2-1065HOC PSYCHOLOGY           A- 0.50  8
66MCG ADV. LANGUAGE S    A  0.50     2-1086HOC SEMINAR IN IDEA      A  0.50  8
04EDW U.S. HISTORY SU    A- 0.50     4-2004EDW U.S. HISTORY SU      A- 0.50  6
44GOT GEOMETRY           A  0.50     5-3144GOT GEOMETRY             A  0.50  6
03JEF PRE-CHEM/PHYSIC    A- 0.50     6-3603JEF PRE-CHEM/PHYSIC      A  0.50  6
76SOR ART SURVEY         A  0.50     3-6643BAU GENERAL EUSINES      A  0.50  9
4 1    TAR  1 SEM  3.8C CR  3.       SEM 2     TAR    SEM       CR  3.
/3 1/2DY AB  6 CK  3.80 CR  3.       92/3 1/2DY AB 14 CF      CR  6.00
                                                    3.833
```

```
  960560 GRAFF REX III          M10   3530 960560 GRAFF REX III          M10
HOC DEBATE               A  0.50     14820PG AM NOVEL SEMINA  B  0.50  3
KET SEM IN THE ESSA      A- 0.50  1  1683KET JOURNALISM       A  0.50  4
EDW PRACTICAL LAW        A  0.50     2002EDW CONSUMER EDUCAT   A- 0.50  5
FLO ALGEBRA II           A- 0.50     3123FLO ALGEBRA II       A  0.50  5
DYK BIOLOGY I            A  0.50     3724DYK BIOLOGY I         A  0.50  3
SZC PHY. ED/HEALTH       A  0.50  1  7003SZC PHY. ED/HEALTH   A+ 0.50  3
    TAR  1 SEM  3.88 CR  3.00        SEM 2     TAR    SEM  3.77 CR  3.00
 1/2DY AB  1 CM  3.85 CR  9.00       93/4 1/2DY AB  8 CM  3.83 CR 12.00
```

Economics							
Geography							

Rather boring records,
like report cards,
can be spiced up
with edit cards.
Note highlighting.

HONORS

College Prep

Instrumental
Vocal

Gyr
Swi

Bus
Boc
Shc
Typ

Shc
Dra
Agr

ACADEMICS

I enjoy high school and the activities it
provides. Sometimes challenge and motivation are
hard to find while sitting up at 1:30 pouring over
Algebra II again, but because of a grade point's
importance and the people who may depend on my
competence one day to bring home the paycheck, I
persevere.

Rex Graff uses statistical sheets in two ways.
This page, a formal transcript of grades,
gives the reader an idea of his overall
academic performance.

Dr
Lit

Attendance Summary

Previous School

Authorized By:

Signed: _____

Position: _____

Date: _____

WORK IN PROGRESS

Individual Statistics
UNOFFICIAL 1994 ELKS VARSITY

RUSHING

o	Name	Att	Gain	Loss	Net	Ave	TD
	T. THIBERT	132	749	36	713	5.4	8
	R. GRAFF	110	554	2	552	5.0	7
	J. VELIQUETTE	71	312	23	289	4.1	3
	J. WILSON	14	44	0	44	3.1	0
	M. SCHAUB	5	39	0	39	7.8	0
	R. O'DONNELL	4	14	0	14	3.5	0
	C. BEATY	28	30	48	-18	-.6	1

An orignal idea: Including a sports stat sheet. This might show a balance, that the good student is not a grind.

PASSING

o	Name	Comp	Att	Pct	Int	Yds	TD
	C. BEATY	31	135	22.9	13	361	0
	J. VELIQUETTE	1	4	25.	0	5	0
	D. DINSMORE	0	3	20	0	0	0

PUNTS

No	Name	No	Ave
90	J. ELLIS	19	36.3
34	T. THIBERT	5	29

KICKOFFS

No	Name	No	Ave
55	T. ZAK	31	33.8

RECEIVING

No	Name	No	Yds	Ave	TD
90	J. ELLIS	12	177	14.75	0
40	J. VELIQUETTE	8	96	12.	0
34	T. THIBERT	6	51	8.5	0
	R. GRAFF	6	19	3.2	0

PUNT RETURNS

No	Name	No	Yds	Ave
34	T. THIBERT	5	88	17
22	R. O'DONNELL	1	8	8
80	J. WILSON	1	7	7
10	D. DINSMORE	1	5	5
	No Return	20		

KICKOFF RETURNS

No	Name	No	Yds	Ave
40	J. VELIQUETTE	7	72	10
34	T. THIBERT	5	94	18
88	B. PRICE	4	52	13
	R. GRAFF	4	47	11
44	M. SCHAUB	2	24	12
22	R. O'DONNELL	1	30	30
10	D. DINSMORE	1	2	2
	No Return	12		

INTERCEPTIONS

No	Name	No	Yd
44	M. SCHAUB	3	3.
60	J. LAKE	1	2.

This page shows his impressive football statistics, rushing, tackles, etc. which, with his strong academic performance and activities, prove him to be an all-around man indeed.

TACKLES

o	Name	UT	AT	TOT
	J. VELIQUETTE	19	60	79
	R. GRAFF	28	44	72
	T. THIBERT	17	39	56
	C. BEATY	16	24	40
	T. ZAK	9	31	40
	J. BAROY	14	22	36
	J. ELLIS	12	23	35
	J. LAKE	7	28	35
	M. SCHAUB	10	16	26
	J. MERCHANT	7	17	24
	S. GLICK	2	11	13
	B. PRICE	3	9	12
	S. MacDONALD	3	8	11
	J. RUSSELL	1	10	11
	J. WILSON	0	9	9
	K. RENWICK	2	5	7
	D. DINSMORE	3	3	6
	J. CROLL	0	5	5
	A. RAYBURN	0	3	3
	R. O'DONNELL	0	3	3

FUMBLE RECOVERIES

No	Name	No
	R. GRAFF	3
	J. MERCHANT	2
60	J. LAKE	2
90	J. ELLIS	2
40	J. VELIQUETTE	1
70	J. RUSSELL	1
55	T. ZAK	1
10	D. DINSMORE	1

SCORING

No	Name	Tot
34	T. THIBERT	58
	R. GRAFF	44
40	J. VELIQUETTE	26
	C. BEATY	6
44	M. SCHAUB	6
60	J. LAKE	6
88	P. PRICE	2
22	R. O'DONNELL	1

BLOCKED KICKS

No	Name	No
3.	R. GRAFF	1
60	John Lake	1

1994 SEASON RECORD . 3 - 6

9/2	KALKASKA	14	ELKS	13
9/9	KINGSLEY	16	ELKS	0
9/16	BOYNE CITY	24	ELKS	12
9/23	HARBOR SPRINGS	12	ELKS	35
9/30	CHARLEVOIX	14	ELKS	8
10/8	CENTRAL LAKE	12	ELKS	28
10/14	EAST JORDAN	28	ELKS	14
10/21	ONAWAY	26	ELKS	27
10/28	T.C. ST. FRANCIS	34	ELKS	12

TEAM SCORING

	1ST	2ND	3RD	4TH	TOTAL	AVE.
ELKS	20	32	56	41	149	16.6
OPP.	46	74	26	34	180	20.0

TEAM YARDAGE

	RUSHING	AVE.	PASSING	AVE.
ELKS	1633	181.4	366	40.7
OPP.	1561	173.4	690	76.7

Showing Yourself Creatively

Show your special creativity in your portfolio. The tongue-in-cheek poem below shows the student's sense of humor about his participation in sports along with his poetic talent.

Other students have used photographs of their three-dimensional art, sketches of Halloween costumes, and diagrams of their personalities in various forms. Spend time thinking of the various ways you can represent yourself!

Sutter's Hill

Oh, we're running cross the country,
It's fall in Michigan.
We're running hard and training hard,
Determined we will win.

Our coach's name is Edwardson;
He wants us to run hard.
He takes us out to Sutter's Hill,
And watches from his car.

There is no steeper real estate
East of the Mississippi.
That hill's so high it scrapes the sky;
No lie, I'll bet my bippy.

Yes, Sutter's Hill is quite a threat,
Approaching a right angle,
By the time you get up to the top,
Your legs you must untangle.

Once a week we go to Sutter's,
And how our muscles strain!
Yes, once a week we venture out
In snow or sleet, or rain.

We run, we sweat, we strain and cuss,
We creep and crawl, and still . . .
Heaven ain't as hard to reach,
As the top of Sutter's Hill.

- - Dave Ketchum

Always Starting at the Bottom

With a simple line drawing and stick figures, Jay Manley, *Super Student's* production manager, represents his indomitable, "I'll tackle anything!" philosophy.

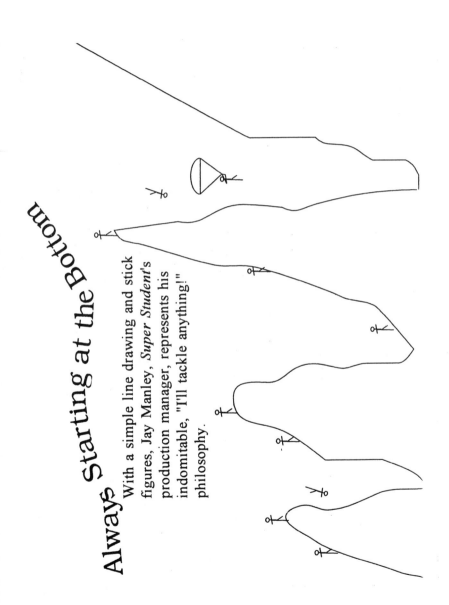

Appendix D

Active Listening Dialog

Principle: The active listener repeats, nearly word for word, what the speaker says.

Purpose: This demonstrates that the listener is, indeed, listening. It gives the speaker time to re-think and possibly reassess his thoughts and words. It encourages the speaker to amplify, clarify, or perhaps even change direction, certainly to get his thoughts out fully.

Dialog

John: I am really peeved with Ms. Mudhen, I mean, am I mad!

Jennifer: You're really mad? Totally?

John: Yeah, she wouldn't even accept my paper.

Jennifer: Wouldn't take it, accept it at all?

John: She didn't even look at it... just because it was three days late!

Jennifer: It was three days late, and she wouldn't even look!

John: Yeah. I mean, she made a big deal about deadlines and all, but she took my last paper late.

Jennifer: She *did* emphasize deadlines. So your last paper was late, and she took it, huh?

John: Yeah, I guess I was lucky last time. Not this time, though. Guess I learned a lesson the hard way.

Jennifer: Probably true, but look, if you learned she's serious about this deadline stuff, next time... well....

John: Next time I get it done on time. Remind me, Jenn.

Jennifer: Yeah, I'll remind you. Hey, maybe we can work together!

John: Together? Got yourself a deal.

Appendix E

Thinking on Paper

Brainstorming

General rules of Brainstorming:

1. Anything goes! Do not edit any ideas. Write down all ideas that occur, no matter how stupid, how impractical, or how legal. Even thinking "edit" interferes with the creative process, the flow of ideas. Freedom from editing also encourages piggybacking ideas--an excellent idea might be suggested by a silly one.

2. Do not stop to edit spelling. In fact, you can abbreviate or record in note form, as long as you can later recall your idea.

Brainstorming example:

Question: How many uses can you think of for an 8 inch pot lid?

Brainstormed list:

1.   cover pot
2.   cover dish
4.   cover burner
5   dish (inverted lid)
6.   flower bowl
7.   cup
8.   junk container

9.   fish bowl
10. flower pot
11. cymbal
12. noisemaker (attention getter in an emergency)
13. as a triangle (music)
14. half a megaphone
15. muffler (of sound)
16. cover test answers
17. cover messes
18. hide things
19. make circles
20. cut giant cookies
21. form pancakes
22. weapon (hit)
23. weapon (cut, bruise)
24. frisbee
26. toy, invent games
27. marker in race
28. tool for sand marking/writing
29. making sand castles (scoop)
30. making sand castles (mold)

Comments on list:

1-3.   Answers that are immediately obvious, in fact, the intended functions of the lid.

4. A bit more original, the student probably visualized the stove.

5. Student doesn't find much more on the stove to cover, so he jumps off the stove subject (a plateau) and gets creative, inverting the lid.

5-10. The student brainstorms various uses of the inverted lid. Note he hops around with uses between the related flower bowl and flower pot. Also his vocabulary is working for him as the "dish" (5) becomes "bowl"(6) which suggests new uses.

11-16. Jumps off container plateau into music and sound. Note the ideas go from amplification (megaphone) to muffling sound.

15-18. Muffling, minimizing suggests covering. Again vocabulary suggests transition from "cover" to "hide."

19-21. Back to visualizing. See the lid, seeing the shape, suggests using its shape to trace (19) and go one step further to cut (20) and form (21).

22-24. Drafting uses exhausted, the student jumps into a new area of use: weaponry.

24-27. Various uses of the lid as a weapon in hand lead to the use of the lid as a projectile, which in turn, leads to the frisbee (25) and a whole new category, toys and games.

28-30. Sand suggests more use as a tool, scoop, and mold (which is actually related to No. 21.)

Note: The brainstorming process is more or less the same for an individual and for a group or class working together.

Thinking on Paper

General to Specific: There and Back!

Knowing how to use generalities and specifics, abstractions and concrete entities (things), is an enormously handy tool for writing and thinking. This is how it works:

Plus (+) means broaden the category of the word. Minus (-) means narrow it. Directions are underlined. Here are some simple exercises.

<u>+4</u> our Christmas tree

our Christmas tree (The start: Broaden.)
Christmas trees +1
evergreen trees +2
trees +3
plants +4

<u>- 4 drama</u>
drama (The start: Narrow.)
players -1
actresses -2
character actresses -3
Jodie Foster -4

Practice in thinking inductively (going from a specific idea to a broader concept) and in thinking deductively (beginning with a general idea and focusing down to a specific example) is helpful in writing sentences, paragraphs, and entire papers.

The logical sequence of your thinking will be reflected in the logical development of the ideas you put on paper. In order to write clear term papers, it is important to recognize these patterns, and it is also helpful in creative writing. It adds grace and wit to your work, including personal writing like letters and journals.

Exercise: Look over the following list of examples for the use of the general or abstract and the specific or concrete. You might also want to look up "simile," " metaphor," and "zeugma" in a handbook of literary terms.

A simile: The noon sun was as bright as her imagination.

A metaphor: He held her small, pale wrist; he held confusion.

Zeugma: The general looked hard at the recruit; and, in a moment, the Appalachian lad lost his innocence and the slouch in his posture.

Writing, like music, might contain crescendos, series which become more powerful toward the end: The teacher demanded her students' homework, attention, and souls.

Or, decrescendos which decrease in size: The thief! He took my life savings, my stereo, my shoelaces!

Doodling, fooling around on paper, practicing the use of the general and specific, the abstract and the concrete, can be fun. Try it. It most certainly will improve your speech, your writing, your thinking, and possibly, your life. (Hey ! That's a crescendo!)

A doodle by the author's daughter, Blake, at age 16. A talented sculptor, Ketchum doodles, thinks on paper, and sketches.

MOM:
LAUGH,
LAUGH,
LAUGH!

Cross Keys Inn

The author's late father, G. Fred DeBolt, was an ardent doodler. Here is a 1920's hitchhiker.

BAY CITY MI

COLUMBIA MARYLAND
(301) 730-3900

BALTIMORE MARYLAND
(301) 532-6900

Thinking on Paper

Clustering

Use unlined paper. Lines mean linear thoughts to the brain, clustering is scattershot brainstorming. Start with your subject circled at the center. Jot down whatever comes to your mind while thinking about the subject, in this case, "TEACHERS." Circle each word after you write it to "nail it down." Draw a line from the new circle back to the circle which prompted the idea.

Note that in some cases, one subject (like professors) prompts a new idea (like Einstein). That's fine. Circle and connect to the source idea. You can cluster until you feel either bored or empty. Do not edit because you might piggy back a good idea onto a poor one. Anything goes! If you think it, write it down.

One main function of clustering is to warm up, to get ideas flowing, to increase fluency. I also like to teach students to use their clusters to generate their writing plan, their outline. Sometimes I ask students to use colored markers to group similar or connected ideas. On the following TEACHER cluster, for instance, the kinds of relationships teachers have with students might be marked in red, e. g. "mentors," and "friends." Named teachers might be circled in blue. Then *specific fictional* teachers, like Mr. Chips and those in *Dead Poet's Society* might be double circled in blue. The student then might decide to write a paper comparing and contrasting real and fictional teachers. His thesis might be "Fictional teachers have time to devote to huge problems; real teachers face huge problems and hundreds of time consuming small ones." Make your own teacher cluster, and find possible theses.

A high school student's cluster of "Teachers."

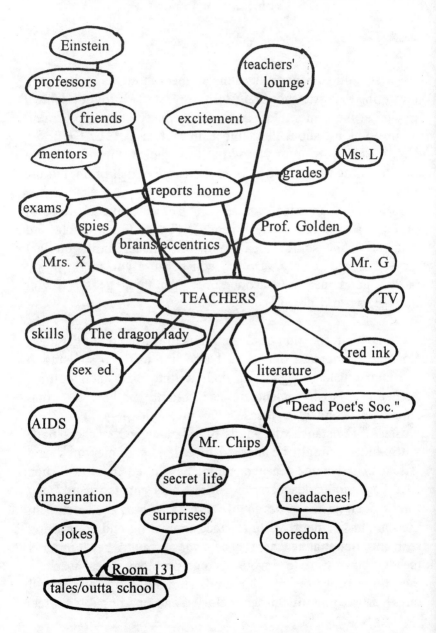

Cluster by Jesse Wilkinson
4th grade Mill Creek Elementary
Williamsburg, Michigan

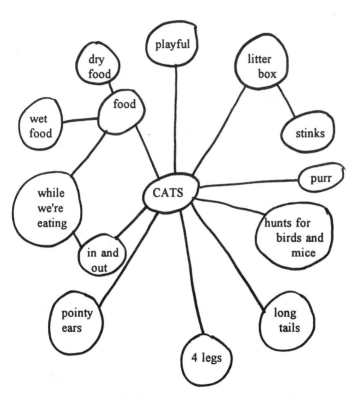

Jesse, who happens to write poetry, could write a poem from this cluster about cats and eating: what they eat, how they eat while the family eats, and how they like to go in and out during dinner.

Or, she might write a poem that shows cats' two sides, playful fellows and the hunters of mice and birds.

Appendix F

Sample Notes

Am. Lit. 10/11/95 - Mr. Phelps

Herman Melville (1819 NY -1891 NY)

dad died...poor...minimal school...19-25, to sea--worked/wrote...obscurity/died

whalers were "my Yale," i.e. education -- self-taught

visited Pacific isles (basis/settings for tales), <u>Typee</u>, <u>Omoo</u>

<u>*Moby Dick*</u> (1850-?)

Period: "Flowering of New England"

... immense talent
... one generation
... one place
... knew each other

M. <u>not</u> a TRANSCENDENTALIST

<u>Transcendentalists</u>	<u>Anti-trans</u>.
Thoreau	Melville
Emerson	Hawthorne
Dickinson (?) not pub. yet	

IDEAS

<u>Transcendentalists</u>	<u>Anti-trans.</u>
one spirit/force	division/disunity
look to nature, find higher laws	dark /light (sun)
OVERSOUL humanity god-like transcending spirit	acknow'd evil human desire vs possibilities

(Both look to nature for evidence of human spirit, but
 they find different things.)

Moby Dick:
Not popular at publication.
Rediscovered 1920's: appreciated
loaded with whaling info
religious themes, symbolism
rich for ideas, quotations, e. g. motley crew, Catskill eagle

M's intention: "monument to the whaling industry"
                but he went deeper ... into mysteries of nature
                "and tragedies of human thought."

135 short chapters

To do:
Buy "Cliff Notes" on <u>Moby</u>, <u>Billy Budd</u>(?)
Get M. bio from media center
Ask Kenesia for Tuesday's notes

Appendix G

Test Taking Tips

An Outline of Test Taking Tips

1. General Preparation

2. Specific Preparation

3. Reading the Test

4. A List of Directional words

5. Planning strategy
   A. Time budget
   B. Survey and check/note

6. Answering individual questions
   A. Plan and note
   B. Write answers

7. Proofreading

NOTE: *Special tips for essay and short answer tests and for math or science tests follow these general directions.*

1. General Preparation

General mental and physical preparation means sleeping well and sleeping enough, eating well and eating enough, and monitoring any prescribed medications you take for derogatory side-effects such as drowsiness or agitation which cause lack of focus.

Good pre-test foods are carbohydrates for staying power and milk products (yogurt, shakes, ice cream) for natural enzymes which relax the nervous system. If you think a candy bar gives you energy, shove one in your pocket, but an apple (or especially a bagel) works better.

2. Specific Preparation

Specific preparation to take a test means Warm-up Thinking and Warm-up Writing. If the actual testing situation leaves you no time for warming up, then do so at home. Do some creative thinking, brainstorm, or do some journal or diary writing. If there is any free time while tests are being distributed, doodle or cluster subject material. Work a couple of equations. However, *never* take time from listening to test instructions and directions to warm-up. Careful, full attention, listening to instructions is critical. Often you'll pick up tips, pointers, and sometimes even answers!

Specific physical preparation means having everything you might possibly need during the exam. You will not only need enough paper (in college, bluebooks), pencils, pens, erasers, white correction fluid, etc., but you may need extra tissue or handkerchiefs, gum, cough drops, etc. Check what is allowed.

Some times, breaks are scheduled in long tests like the SAT or ACT, then you will want to pack fruit or a sandwich and juice to take along.

Be certain to ask ahead of time about such critical matters of academic honesty as what is or is not allowed--books, notes, dictionaries, periodic tables, calculators, etc.

3. Reading the Test

(Specific tips for reading different types of tests are given later in this appendix.)

The importance of reading tests carefully cannot be emphasized enough. This story appears on every campus (There must be a reason.): The student starts with question No. 1 and races against time to finish the long final examination, only to find a direction at the end which states, "Answer only the even numbered questions."

To read a test intelligently:

A. Read any instructions, general or specific, written on the test thoroughly--several times--at least until you feel you understand them completely. If you do not have this confidence or have *any* question, *ask* the teacher or monitor before you begin.

B. Read the entire test (questions) through carefully, and let the material hit your brain. Don't look for what *you* want to be on it or how *you* interpret it. *Let the test talk to you.*

C. Re-read the test (questions) more slowly now, evaluating

questions for level of difficulty for you and importance in overall grade or score. BE SURE TO FIND OUT POINTS OR PERCENTAGE ALLOTTED, IF SO MARKED.

D. Look for directional words and use them.

4. List of Directional Words

analyze	identify	suppose
assess	illustrate	support
chart	indicate	tell
cite	interpret	trace
classify	judge	
comment	justify	
compare	list	
contrast	mention	
criticize	name	
deduce	outline	
describe	propose	
define	prove	
demonstrate	rank	
develop	relate	
diagram	review	
differenitate	show	
distinguish	sketch	
enumerate	state	
evaluate	summarize	

5. Planning Strategy

Basic planning strategy: Survey for TIME BUDGET, Survey for DIFFICULTY, and POINTS/PERCENTAGES.

If you are prepared and the test is of moderate difficulty, making a time budget is simple. Allow 5 minutes for directions and distribution of test materials, subtract 5-10 % of the remaining time (10% minimum for essay tests) for proof-reading, and apportion the remaining time by the number of questions (essay) or sections (short answer).

If the test is more difficult, then more time should be allowed on the questions/problems you can confidently answer. Next, plan time for those questions which you feel you can attempt with some success.   Do not plan to spend time struggling over questions which seem too difficult. If anything, plan time to only jot down some key terms or formulas/methods that might work.

Further, note credit (points/percentages) given for answers, and apportion time logically according to the point value of the questions so that you won't write paragraphs for short answers and run out of time on big (heavy credit) essay questions. If this sounds too difficult, take heart. Planning time budgets for tests becomes easier with practice!

Answering specific questions involves much of the above strategy: Find directional words, e.g. "evaluate." Find key terms, e.g. "symbiotic" or "sonnet." Then, follow the strategies below which are suitable for the type of test, essay or short answer. In either case, take that extra few seconds to prepare yourself physically: Stretch or shake your hands, rotate your neck, take a deep breath, remind yourself this is *your* turn to show your stuff, and then begin.

6. Individual Questions

(See specific test types, essay, short answer, etc.)

7. Proofreading

General proofreading advice includes:

... Include proofreading in your time budget
... Use every allotted moment to work (*Never* turn in test early.)
... Proofread the three major ways:

1. Sense! (Am I making sense? Was Raymond afraid of the dark in his "adulthood" or "adultery?" Does this answer seem correct? Which number makes sense? Five friends for a poker game or 500?)

2. Sentences! (Faulty sentences are a common error. Check for fragments and run-ons. A wise student masters sentences, and gets the problem over with for a lifetime!)

3. Proofread word by word, part by part. Check spelling and word choice; or, in math and science, check operation by operation.

4. Check for omittted key words, "not," "but," etc. that might change your intended meaning.

Essay Tests

All strategies, patterns of exposition (structure), creative writing devices (alliteration, rhythm, etc.), and elements used in essay writing apply--as much as is possible in allowed time--to answering essay questions.

Important: An essay has a THESIS (MAIN POINT). The ANSWER to the QUESTION will be the THESIS/MAIN POINT of your essay.

A middle school example:

> Question: How do hound dogs hunt?
> Thesis of answer: Hounds hunt by smell or sight.

> Or, on a high school or college test,

Example:

> Question: What are the major characteristics of the Romantic period of literature?

> Thesis of answer: The major characteristics of the romantic period are an emphasis on emotion, freedom, appreciation of the individual, love of nature, fascination with the rare or exotic, and a distrust of pure reason.

> In short, an essay answer means that the student should: Pre-write, write, and edit. Pre-writing for essay answers on

tests is merely jotting down elements of the answer on your scratch or work/planning area. I prefer a separate page, although margins will do. College students should write on the right side of bluebook pages, and do pre-writing/planning on the left page. Students have only a very brief time for this when taking tests. Nevertheless, this brief pre-writing and planning is critical.

If you use a separate sheet for outlining, planning, thinking on paper, turn it in. Many teachers will give you credit for this, or at least look more kindly upon your other answers!

While you don't have time for a formal outline, you might jot something down like: "Speilberg's right! Two examples, results, and recap/emphasize." In this case, these eight words will keep you on track as you write the short essay answer.

Again, although you will be pressed for time, you should follow the *Essay Writing Process*. Here is one version of the essay process.

Essay Writing Process

1. Read question thoroughly.
2. Take a minute or two to think without writing.
3. Pre-write (warm up).
4. Write the essay.

A. Introduction (Brief! You may want to put ANSWER (THESIS) first on tests. In literature/language/writing classes, a brief introduction might add grace and points).

B. State THESIS (The direct answer to the presented question.) Your THESIS/ANSWER should take the form of a clear declarative sentence.   Subject--verb--direct object preferred.

C. Develop your thesis through a logical pattern. Frequently this pattern will be determined by directional words in the question. "Compare and contrast," "Exemplify," "Analyze," etc, are all directional words which suggest a pattern of writing to use. Use specific examples to back up generalizations, e. g. "He was a difficult baby to tend; he had long periods of colic and several fevers above 102 degrees." Use your teacher's or book's examples, and then nail down an A with an example of your own.

D. Emphasizing your thesis, re-stating it in new terms, might be a suitable closure for an essay test answer.

E. Proofread. Along with the three basics (sense, sentences, and word by word), read for common errors such as barbarisms (it's/its, alot/a lot), agreement of number, and completeness. (Have you included all that you know?)   Underline key words for emphasis.

Short Answer Tests

A strategy, in a nutshell, for taking short answer tests follows:

1. Read all instructions several times, until you completely understand them. Read instructions for tips.

2. Fill in name and requested information.

3. Survey test for points/credit.

4. Survey test to evaluate difficulty. As rapidly as possible, scan the questions, marking them as follows: + = know it. ✔ = good chance. No mark means that you don't know the answer.

5.   Take the test.
(N. B. Check periodically that answer sheets, if used, are properly aligned with questions.)

6. Proof-read.

7. Check that your name and other requested information is correct.

8. Hand in confidently.

The above system is quite simple. There are tips to take a short answer test for maximum performance.

First, answer all questions marked plus, then answer the checked questions, then attempt the minus questions with remaining time. Always guess if scoring is not right minus wrong.

Consider strategies for working out those you've marked with a check (good chance), and later, intelligently guessing at those questions marked with minuses (don't know it).

Working and Guessing Through Multiple Choice

1.   Attack the question; read it confidently, looking for clues.

2. Read carefully so you don't misinterpret, and don't jump at what seems obvious and fall into possible traps. Fair tests rarely trap students. Traps appear, however, more frequently on teacher-written tests rather than on standardized ones.

3. After you understand the question, propose an answer in your own mind, and search the choices for a similar one.

4. Consider *all* choices before you commit to an answer.

5. Sometimes you can narrow the number of choices by discarding those that don't seem to answer the question directly? For instance: *Eggplant is frequently used in Mediterranean recipes because:*

A. It's purple   B. It grows in the region   C. It's oblong

All answers are true of eggplant, but only B answers the question.

6. Consider directional words like "always," "rarely/seldom," and "never" seriously. Note that they are specific; they mean exactly what they mean.

7. Use logic and instinct. Using logic means pitting one choice against the other, which choices are similar and why? Which is the more specific? Do you see a pattern among the choices you know to be correct or incorrect?

Perhaps you can piggyback an answer. Consider...

Question: Which of the following are common to dogs?

A. Four legs
B. Pink tongues
C. glomerular membranes
D. All of the above
E. None of the above

In spite of the fact that the student does not know that glomerular membranes are tiny capillary vessels in the kidneys of all dogs, logic will show him D is the correct answer. Instinct is important. Never change your first guess unless the truly correct answer has come to mind.

Math and Science Tests

As when taking other tests, students should use basic good methods:
1. Come well prepared and rested.
2. Read through the test carefully, noting instructions.
3. Budget your time intelligently.
4. Attack individual questions.
5. Check your work.

General Preparation Strategies

1. Sharpen the tools that you know you are likely to need: If your homework in the course has included use of fractions or trigonometiric identities or exponential numbers and those tools are a bit rusty, be sure to sharpen those skills as part of your study program for the exam. Younger students should review multiplication tables, principles, and procedures in their textbooks.

2. If the test will entail using formulas and you have trouble

remembering them, use flash cards in your study and give them one last review in the hall before the exam. Then walk in, sit down, and immediately write out your list of key formulas from memory on the margin of the test paper. (For obvious reasons, college students should not write the formulas on the bluebooks they bring to class.)

3. When you do your homework and prepare for the test, don't solve problems by rote. *Think the process through* each time so that you *understand why* you simplify or combine or reduce or cancel or substitute.

4. Know your Learning Style (See LEARNING STYLES) and put it to work in your preparation for tests: If you are an aural/oral learner, say what you are doing as you review material and solve problems. If you are a visual learner, make charts, posters of formulas and diagrams, and paste them in your study area so that they become well imprinted in your visual memory. If you are a kinesthetic learner, take a cue from rap music and combine oral expression and memorization with a bit of physical rhythm.

5. Have your estimating skills in good order. Think questions through in simple round numbers in your head--then crunch the full numbers and compare. Especially in courses where digital calculators are allowed or even required, a well estimated answer is your only protection against missed key strokes.

6. Become good at reading and sketching graphs and diagrams of all sorts.

Critical Strategies for Math and Science Tests

A. Short Answer/True/False, Matching Questions

1. Read carefully and quickly answer what you know for sure. Leave the rest for later. What you can't recall immediately will likely resurface in the course of the exam and you can come back for a break.

2. As a rule, trust your first answer unless you are sure later that it is dead wrong.

B. Multiple Choice Questions

1. Solve problems first in your head--then look for the best answer. Eliminate the obviously wrong choices.

2. Check to see if the logical answer is expressed in a different form among the test choices.

3. If you're stuck, try working backwards from the answers: Which answer would most logically come from what was asked in the question?

C. Full Questions

Here's some data; this is the question; you figure out what to do and crank out an answer (which had better be right or else you lose all your points, your good grade, your college scholarship, and any shot you ever had at happiness and a credit card)! Sometimes tests make you feel like this. Yikes! Well, take heart, it isn't that bad in the real world, at least not often. Remember that this book teaches that *tests are your chance to show your stuff*. Attack the problem.

1. Look for the basic principles involved and begin to get the data into consistent units. If the problem looks easier in the metric system, convert your foot-pounds into newton-meters and your quarts and pints into liters.

2. Diagram the event or process and add dimensions--quantify the occurrence.

3. Don't expect the problem to be a total stumper from end to end, but do look for some of the quirky stuff that was in the more difficult homework problems (which an ideal student would do and review as part of his preparation).

4. Look for information that may be irrelevant. And try to analyze the remaining data without the possible red herring. Occasionally you may actually have a sequence of fairly simple problems mixed together.

5. If nothing seems to work, still note what forumla, law, or theorem you believe is involved. Show all your work. Even if the answer is incorrect, you may get partial credit.

Appendix H

Bonus Red Hot Tips

1. Find the best of all possible (for you) inexpensive pens and pencils and use them in school. Leave expensive pens at home; you'll lose them. Keep a wide variety of writing implements on hand at home.   Having them encourages writing.   Spoil yourself.

2. Butcher paper, shelf paper, paper bags, etc. can serve as art paper for youngsters.

3. Keep a thick notebook for each separate class, and an extra one for personal stuff.

4. Quart size zip-shut plastic bags keep textbooks which go back and forth between home and school in good condition. This should be a must if the book is a fine volume or if you intend to keep the book in your permanent library.

5. Unless you are in art, use only black or dark blue ink for academic work. Save the exotic colors for personal fun.

6. Wheel, deal, do everything on the good side of ethical to try to get the best lab partner in class. All's fair in love and lab partners.

7. Do NOT build a sentimental shrine to teddy bears, boy-girlfriends, or summer memories on a bulletin board near your study place. Keep up-beat, invigorating, motivational stuff there.

8. If possible, sit near the smartest kids in class. Give one a sheet of carbon paper (that old-fashioned blue/black stuff). Make a deal that if one of you is absent, the other will "carbon copy" class notes that day.

9. Write the phone number of a smart classmate in your notebook the first day of class. You can get help or assignments if you are absent.

10. In a new class, be rather low-profile/quiet the first three days of class until you learn what style your teacher likes.

11. Save the romance for romantic places.

12. Find out whether your teacher likes to be called "Mrs.," "Ms.," " Mr., " " Dr.," " Sir," or "Hey, Jose!"

13. Never hold up your teacher before or after class with a lengthy problem. "Is there a quiz tomorrow?" is a question that is just long enough. You *may* ask *when* you can talk to him later.

14. Don't become involved (take sides) in teacher to teacher spats.

15. If you goof, even really big, admit it (perhaps privately) fully, honestly, and openly to the teacher.

16. Never call a teacher at home. If it is life or death, call 911.

17. Give teachers *honest* compliments now and then. They're human, really.

18. Learn the difference between the active and passive voice. (Yes, you'll have to study this a bit, but it is well worth it.) Use the forceful active voice in your work as much as possible.

19. Use verbs. Adjectives are an easy way out, but they are wimpy.

20. Be clean. A little messy is usually ok.

21. Keep your language clean. Profanity and purposeless vulgarity have no place in the academe.

22. Be timely. Keep attendance up.

23. Special favors are not due because you've been absent.

24. Thank the teacher for a good class.

25. If something is important, write it*, don't say it. The written word carries much weight. *"I love you." is the exception. Don't write "I love you." in notes. You'll probably change your mind by 5th hour class.

26. Never, ever, sleep in class.

27. If you have a bad (contagious) cold, stay home.

28. Cookies may be given for sprained ankles or smashed thumbs, but academic favors are not due.

29. Play to your strength. If you're good at art, ask if you can

illustrate (not skip) your book report. If you are a poet, write a poem about barium for chemistry. One biology teacher got a soft-sculpture of the DNA double helix from a kid who sewed.

30. If you play mind games with your teacher, you may win, but the teacher has the grade book.

31. Writing *clear* prose comes before political correctness, regardless of your feelings on the gender issue. When writing, use the third person singular (he, him, himself, etc.)--unless you are writing about lingerie, giving birth, or the women's movement. "He/she," "he or she," etc. often just muddies up your work. (Of course, an exception is when a teacher demands a different usage and you are captive in his class.) If in doubt, aim for clarity.

32. If you can get a series (a mini-list, e. g. apathy, greed, egotism, etc.) into a THESIS (Apathy, greed, and egotism caused the fall of Dictator Dupe.), it will easily fall apart into an outline, the game plan for your paper. Outline:

Introduction/THESIS
Dupe's apathy
Dupe's greed
Dupe's egotism
Conclusion

33. Keep some music (No lyrics!) special for study, if you must have music.

34. Never be the first one to hand in a test.

35. Keep your pencils sharp. You might prefer inexpensive, disposable automatic pencils; then sharpening is not a problem.

36. An automatic pencil sharpener is a boon in the home study area. Ask for one as a holiday or birthday gift. You won't regret it.

37. Young women: Practice basic feminine manners in the classroom. It is not a place to apply make-up, hair spray, or nail polish.

38. Everyone: Manners! Do not comb hair, take off shoes, or put feet on the desk tops, tables, or other people in class.

39. If you have a bad cough, control it, or ask to leave the room. Usually a piece of hard candy works just as well as a cough drop. Remember some cough medicines make students sleepy.

40. Don't pass notes in class, yours or anyone else's. If someone hands you one, shake your head, "No," and don't accept it.

41. Smart students don't chew gum, allowed or not.

42. Keep tissue or a handkerchief handy.

43. Forgetting your textbooks is a cardinal sin.

44. Burying your papers in the pile when you turn them in signals the teacher that you are ashamed of your work. The teacher thinks it must be awful, and he hasn't even seen it!

45. If you're uptight or nervous or feel a bad day coming on, wear clean, loose, comfortable clothing.

46. Don't flirt with teachers, even when kidding.

47. If you make some terrible mistake or have an embarrassing accident, admit it, say, "I'm sorry." once, clearly, and forget about it.

48. Privately inform the teacher if you know of cheating. If you cannot bring yourself to name names, don't. But do inform the teacher that "nameless" kids are copying, cheating, whatever.

49. Don't talk too fast in class, especially when giving a formal speech or presentation. Pause and take a breath now and then. Most students speak too rapidly if they are nervous.

50. When you speak make eye contact with several people in the room, including the teacher.

51. Make smiling (sincerely) a habit.

52. Respect confidentiality. Try to keep secrets.

53. Gossip is a potent poison.

54. Never repeat anything that might harm a person's reputation.

55. Be very cautious about humor which involves other people's physical characteristics. Many students cry privately.

56. Never turn in work with food (or strange unidentified) stains.

57. Throwing away homework or tests within the teacher's sight is a bad policy.

58. A barbarian is an uneducated, uncivilized rough neck. Dumb, uneducated mistakes (confusion about alot/a lot, its/it's, there/their/they're) are called "barbarisms." Learn the correct use and spellings of these!

59. If you have an opinion that is different from the teacher's, state his first, showing that you have listened. Then take exception, and state your reasons.

60. Control physical habits like hair twisting, finger drumming, etc. as well as you can.

61. Check your posture now and then.

62. If you don't feel well, and want to put your head down, quietly ask the teacher first.

63. If you borrow a stamp, pay the loaner back with a stamp, not money.

64. Build up a store of good board games, ones that involve wit, creativity, and intelligence. Think it over: These are usually the most fun!

65. If you need a teacher to mail something (a recommendation or application, etc.), always give a stamped, addressed (with a typewriter) envelope when you make the request.

66. SASE means Self-Addressed Stamped Envelope.

67. Get to know the school secretary well. Her help is usually invaluable.

68. Get to know the school librarian well. Her help is usually invaluable.

69. Stick your head in the counselor's office now and then and say hello so he knows you well and you are "on his mind." You never know when you'll need him.

70. Get "the word" on teachers you have not had, so you can consider their style, knowledge, and personality if you have any voice in choosing courses.

71. If you decorate lockers, use good taste. Vulgarity and obscenity are out of place in the school, and they will offend teachers, even if students are accustomed to such stuff.

72. Be especially friendly to school board members if you meet them.

73. Don't join clubs just because your friends are in them. Join because you are interested in the subject or cause.

74. Go out of your way to meet and befriend foreign-exchange students. You'll be the one enriched!

75. Read a newspaper daily; at least scan the headlines, sports, and comics.

76. Don't wear T-shirts or sweats with offensive legends, no matter how funny. You want good grades, not laughs.

77. Don't offend your teacher by knocking his alma mater.

78. Don't argue with people about their personal religious beliefs.

79. If a friend dumps problems on you that are over your head, tell a counselor. At a minimum, tell a parent.

80. If you don't understand something in class, after trying, after studying, tell the teacher. Don't pretend. A law student says this is the most important tip in this book!

81. Never lie about academic matters.

82. Never change a grade.

83. Never forge a parental signature (for you or for a friend).

84. Supposedly one learns not to throw things in a classroom in kindergarten.

85. No walkmans in class (Sorry!).

86. Writing on desks, walls, or carpets is vandalism.

87. Gum is properly trashed with paper (and it goes in the basket, and you shouldn't have it to begin with).

88. If you want a favor of the teacher, ask. Whining, pestering, and begging put you in a bad light.

89. Again, remember kindergarten? Don't run in halls, and do carry scissors and sharp objects safely. Those rules last a life-time.

90. Bringing surprises and treats (boa constrictors or brownies) to class without prior teacher permission is a bad idea.

91. The teacher's classroom is sacrosanct, ask before you change anything.

92. Don't hassle the teacher as soon as he enters the room. Start-up time is necessary.

93. Never leave the classroom until it is obvious that the teacher has dismissed the class. Never, *ever*, rise to leave (even at the bell) if the teacher is still talking.

94. If you want a conference, ask the teacher what time to talk is most convenient for the *teacher*, and then *be there* on time!

95. Inform and remind your parents of parent-teacher conferences and encourage them to go. Such talks always help (whether or not you believe it).

96. Don't go along to parent-teacher conferences unless doing so is usual at your school.

97. Don't complain about one teacher to another. If you have a serious problem with the teacher and cannot talk it over with that teacher, see the counselor or the principal.

98. Don't be late. If you are unavoidably late, enter the room quietly.

99. Inform your teacher of broken equipment.

100. You don't need polished apples. Tell your teachers to "Have a pleasant day." or "Hope your evening's nice." instead.

101. Beware of asking the teacher personal questions.

102. When inter-acting with handicapped friends and classmates, take cues from them about how they wish to be treated. There is such a thing as help and also such a thing as cruel kindness.

103. Study the literary device called "oxymoron." (This has nothing to do with dumb cows.) An oxymoron, like "cruel kindness," is a phrase made of opposite words which gives the meaning power and poetic tension. Examples: "Sweet-sour pork," " icy hot liniment, " "honest politician (?)"!

104. Never touch things on a teacher's desk unless you have permission and there is a reason.

105. Be kind to geeks.

106. Learn what teachers' hobbies are, and chat with teachers about them.

107. If you drive, don't hot rod around the school parking lot.

108. Hood surfing kills.

109. Help, even in small ways, to celebrate the holidays in school-- every holiday, including others' birthdays.

110. If you buy lunch, get to know the lunch ladies! Big helpings and special cuts on the way. Try it!

111. Be your own cheerleader.

112. Don't eat in class.

113. Be brave about reporting illegal activities in school. You may end up saving a situation or even a life.

114. Don't damage library books or periodicals (or steal them).

115. Be aware that strange behavior in your classmates can be caused by many things that you are unaware of (besides drugs).

116. If you think a teacher is stressed, tell the counselor or the principal.

117. Never, ever, put up with harassment of any kind from a teacher or classmate. *Report it immediately.*

118. Valuables are best left home.

119. Classmates may rely on you for study help to some extent, but make it clear that they should do their own work.

120. Eat lunch every day.

121. If you have to miss a meeting tell the sponsor teacher ahead of time. If you can't, remember to apologize as soon as possible.

122. Wear a watch.

123. Keep a calendar.

124. Keep an address book.

125. Keep an assignment book or one place to record assignments.

126. Underline key terms, especially on a test.

127. If the class is interrupted, keep quiet.   Don't use the interruption as "get-crazy" time.

128. If a lesson is lagging, volunteer. Help the teacher save it.

129. Compliment teachers on well-written, fair exams.

130. If you get into an awkward situation where you seem to know more than the teacher (or are handling something more intelligently), back off gracefully. Know-it-alls don't come in first.   If you must correct the teacher, do so quietly and privately.

131. Doodling with loops, drawing tornadoes and slinkies, sometimes frees up rigidity and improves handwriting.

132. If you have very large handwriting (which sometimes looks rather juvenile), get some loose leaf paper from an office supply store which has smaller spaces between lines. This might save a couple of trees, too.

133. If your school tends toward cliques, "cross-clique." Cultivate a group of friends for each class and activity. Mix the groups up, and be open about doing so. Exclusivity is stupid.

134. Form study groups of good students and/or enthusiastic friends.

135. Give out invitations privately. Feelings get hurt.

136. Think about long phone calls: The household of the receiver (and the receiver's parents) is being tied up.

137 Class clowns don't deserve encouragement.

138. Wearing distracting clothes or reacting to the distracting clothing others wear is bad form.

139. If there's no seating chart, stay away from class talkers; or, privately ask to be moved.

140. Read foreign authors who write in English or get translations. Younger students should try C. S. Lewis and Tolkien. Foreign authors often give us new perspectives. Some wonderful stuff is coming from Hispanic, African, and Asian authors.

141. Be brave about mixing personalities in class group work. Lead, and play to each individual's strength.

142. The rear corners of a classroom are losers' corners, spots unintentionally neglected by most teachers. Ask to move if assigned such a seat.

143. Treat the school's and the teacher's equipment with care.

144. There are 144 items in a gross. That's 12 dozen. Isn't that gross? Learn the vocabulary of numbers. Look up "googol."

145. Every time you go to the library, spend 10 minutes "browsing" to look, to survey, to check out new stuff, and find out interesting things about the old.

146. Ask teachers and librarians what their favorite reads (books, newspapers, and periodicals) are.

147. Get to know the school custodians. They are usually great folks and full of interesting stuff to teach you.

148. Don't act up on school busses or field trips.

149. Keep something living near your homework area, a plant or an aquarium. Let your dog or cat nap near you when studying.

150. This mark (.) is called a "period" in most classes. It can be called a "bullet" in journalism. Two, vertically, (:) are called a "colon." Three (...) are called an "ellipsis," a mark of punctuation which means something is left out or the creative writer is marking a pause. Four dots (....) are an "ellipsis" followed by a "period", marking the end of a sentence. Three dots in an upward facing triangle (∴) is a symbol meaning "therefore." Enough to make you dotty?

151. When first viewing art, don't make snap judgments. Study it carefully and mentally *list what you see* in the picture, (tree, grass, sky, moon, lady, etc.) before you start analyzing it. This way you won't miss as much, and you'll have a list of things to analyze in the work.

152. Get the correct spelling of a new teacher's name down first thing, first class.

153. If you don't know the room (teacher's) rules, find out.

154. Try making a model of something unusual. Represent a short story, a grammatical point, a period of history, or a Mobius strip with a model.

155. Don't schedule a medical or dental appointment during school unless it is totally unavoidable. Don't even *think* about scheduling a hair cut during school!

156. Save to buy a comfortable, business-like (office type) chair for your study area. It will be a start toward college dorm furniture, too.

157. Get to know a clerk (or owner) of a good bookstore, large or small.

158. Wash your hands frequently and well during the school day. You'll look better, and the habit is number one way to prevent head colds. Ask any school nurse!

159. Be economical (environmentally wise!) about supplies. A large can of rubber cement and one can of thinner is much more inexpensive than many small jars. Ink fills pens, and some laser printer cartridges can be re-filled.

160. TV's *Wheel of Fortune*'s "megawords" really aren't very challenging. Choose some of your own, and learn how to spell them: You'll have fun and delight people. Examples: "Paraphernalia," "existentialism," "supercilious," etc.

161. Keep an extra shirt and jeans in your locker. Accidents, in art or chemistry, even in the hall, happen.

162. Seriously think about layering your school clothes. Some heating systems are erratic, and weather changes. It is very

difficult to study when you are too cold or hot, especially too hot. Keep an extra sweater in your locker.

163. Keep some stamps in your wallet.

164. Don't flash grades around (good or bad), and don't hide good ones either.

165. If you must leave class, leave quietly and don't loiter on your errand.

166. See your counselor/teacher for scheduling, getting competition blanks, admission papers, etc. *at first opportunity*, as early as possible.

167. Procrastination is an Academic Cardinal Sin.

168. If you feel absolutely overwhelmed by school (and this means *absolutely*--you are sick from it!), stay home *one* day to rest, eat well, sleep, change your mind set, clean up your act, get organized, and study. Remember, while this might be emergency care, it *is* contrary to the "Regular attendance makes good students." rule.

169. Don't cultivate the friendship of vulgar kids. They usually aren't good students or good friends. If you want to help them, be a refined role model.

170. Never trash anything *anywhere* but in the proper place, waste-basket, recycle bin, disposal, etc.

171. Handwriting is generally set by high school years. If you have poor hand-writing, type (or use a computer) *whenever*

possible. When this is not possible, use lots of space and pray.

172. Use good table manners in the cafeteria or at the pizzeria. Think of good manners as being sophisticated and intriguing! Some kids I know practice at a table before prom dinners.

173. Use your wildest imagination when trying to find things in the library. Practice brainstorming synonyms and related ideas to work with card catalogs, *Reader's Guide to Periodicals,* other guides, and cross-indexes. For instance, a Mark Twain quotation about rulers in this book was found under "High Position."

174. Realize that there *are* double standards, i.e. You cannot get away with something others do. For instance, many newspapers and magazines are now dropping commas because their policy is "less punctuation is less clutter." Your school (and certainly universities) will see this issue differently.

175. Students are targets to "con," to take advantage of, since they do, in fact, spend much money. Check out various honors to see if they are true honors, or merely a certificate any student can get by sending in $29.95. Ask a journalism teacher about the "vanity press" and review the various "Who's Who" honors programs. They usually are "fill in the blank and pay." Sophisticated people realize this, and accepting such an honor will backfire. To prove this to one class we put my dog, Red Rover, through such a program. The students answered his questions by rolling dice. He did very well! He still gets mail.

176. Graduation time is expensive enough with the necessities. Consider if you really need all the paraphernalia (extra invitations, seals, lavalieres, etc.) before you spend money on items that will be wasted.

177. Look up the seven deadly sins (You might even think about them.) Such trivia is interesting and comes in handy.

178. Look up and memorize the Wonders of the World, ancient and modern. This is also handy information.

179. Do crossword puzzles (Beyond word search!) at least once a month.

180. Practice your signature (Artists do!) until you get one you rather like. This is good for self-esteem.

181. Among your books, always have two special ones: One that you are reading and one that you would like to read next.

182. Get to know yourself intellectually: Know not only who your favorite musician is, but what kind of music you like best. Not only who your favorite poet is, but what period of literature you like best. Not only who your favorite artist is, but the characteristics of his or her period. You'll discover you are a very interesting person!

183. When you are lucky enough to be among academic angels, to hear a poet read his work, to hear an accomplished musician play, to hear a keen-thinking economist explain his views-- listen, listen, listen! (See LISTENING and NOTES.)

184. Never pretend to knowledge, i.e act as if you know something you don't or are an expert in a field when you are not.

185. If you take a foreign language (*And that is a good idea!*), find a foreign exchange student or someone who speaks that language as a first language, and listen well.

186. When you take a very demanding schedule, you may need some classes that are less demanding. Nevertheless, among the less demanding or time consuming, choose the one best suited to you, your needs, and your goals. Don't take a class just because it is easy. Wasting time feels lousy and is just plain stupid.

187. Cardinal numbers indicate quantity, e. g. 7 or 11.

188. Ordinal numbers indicate order, e.g. 7th or 11th.

189. Learn the right way to plant a tree.

190. Wear bright colors once in a while, even if just a bandana for an accent.

191. If you must protest or take up a cause because of your considered beliefs, do so non-violently.

192. Think green. Think environmentally in every course, in every possible academic endeavor. Write about environment, study ecology, write green poems and paint green art. *That you recycle and support your school's recycling goes without saying!* This book is printed on recycled paper, of course!

193. If you are aware of any weapon in school, report it immediately, even if anonymously. Leave your own pea shooter home; and, yes, snowballs are dangerous.

194. Be sincere in all you do; this includes not kidding yourself. Insincerity wastes time and resources and never leads you to a lasting or worthy goal anyhow.

195. Find out what a shaggy dog story (joke) is. Practice telling shaggy dogs stories and other jokes.

196. Learn to juggle: A rosy path to hand-eye coordination, a lot of fun, and instant popularity. One expert juggler says it even leads to inner peace.

197. Once in a while suspend your disbeliefs in Santa Claus, fairies, leprechauns, and gremlins. "The gremlins did it!" is an especially face-saving line.

198. Learn how to wrap a gift competently, and use your imagination to do it inexpensively! Use comics. Think recycle.

199. Keep young children and babies in your life through occasional or frequent-as-possible contact.

200. Plant something fun, strange, historic, or exotic. Thompson & Morgan, Inc. (an English company) has seeds for them all. Call (908) 363-2225 for an American catalog.

201. Ideally, routines include a *family* reading time. Everyone reads. It doesn't matter what the material is.

202. *The American Heritage Dictionary of the English Language*--Third Edition (New York: Houghton Mifflin Co.) is a wonderful reference book. Reviewers love it!

203. Check libraries and bookstores for displays, new books, best sellers, specialty areas, specialized bibliographies, etc.

204. Wear comfortable clothing, not only for studying, but also for important (long!) exams.

205. If the family watches TV, check the Public TV listings for quality educational and cultural programming. Parents can use television as a springboard for reading.

206. Each family member should have a personal library, however small.

207. Homes should have special libraries, according to family interests, e.g. cookbooks, music, sports, wood-working, etc.

208. Every home should have a reference library, a shelf for dictionaries, a thesaurus, encyclopedias, etc.

209. Develop a system to record book loaning and borrowing.

210. Parents can use reading as a reward: "If you do the job, I'll read a story." or "You may stay up a while to read." To make sure the youngest children get enough sleep, start the bedtime-reading ritual earlier.

211. Parents and older siblings can let young children read to them while they are doing chores, washing dishes, etc.

212. Family members and friends should make an effort to talk about books and about reading. Be enthusiastic.

213. Each family member should have an up-to-date library card for local libraries. Is there a college library near you?

214. Students have often asked, "How can I tell if I am in love?" Mature, adult love makes you feel strong and healthy. You feel free, and you care for what is best for *both* people. Infatuation is when you feel "love sick," and wish to be with the other person constantly, thinking of nothing but your "love" and owning the beloved. Most teen guidance books cover the subject quite well. Check the library for such books. Reading about "courtly love" in a good encyclopedia is also interesting when you want to learn more about love.

215. Tell family stories as well as stories and jokes that you've enjoyed hearing from others and those you've read.

216. Parents should encourage children to talk about stories being read. They should ask open-ended questions. "What do you think about...?"

217. Ask good readers what they are reading. Ask good students what books they like and why.

218. On tests, "true" means the case is *always* true.

219. Don't take medication to relax you for tests. You'll lose important motivation and mental quickness.

220. Don't take medications to pep you up for tests. You'll feel hyper and lose your power to concentrate and focus.

221. If you feel rage, even anger, write it out in a letter and then destroy the letter.

222. Learn how to play checkers, then chess.

223. Choose your extra-curricular activities carefully and sincerely, and work for them. In return, the activities will work for you, giving you pleasure and reward. Don't join anything just to be on the team or in the club.

224. All thinking skills have their places in scholarship. Obviously the higher levels are superior. However, there will be situations when one skill is more suitable to use than another. Free-thinkers, like the main characters in *Dead Poets' Society* (film), will mostly use synthesis and evaluation. But you need to acquire knowledge and comprehension, the lower thinking skills, or all you'll ever be is a gadfly.

225. Some research suggests that girls are very receptive to logic and learning abstract principles of mathematics about 4th grade. The research also suggests that boys are receptive about 7th grade. Parents should expose 8 and 9 year old girls to logic and creative mathematics. They would do well to buy books with puzzles, syllogisms, and Venn diagrams at a teacher's supply store for their daughters and sons at the respective receptive ages.

226. Come to meetings with writing supplies, and set your paper and pencils out before you. Like body language, this act sends powerful signals. Your visible supplies define your space and say clearly that you are prepared to make things happen. As good ideas are presented, jot them down. As the meeting goes along, you might say something like, "I've been making a list of some of the good ideas I've heard (Read them, perhaps adding some ideas of your own!)." Yes! You have just emerged as a leader.

227. Collect something unusual: Ukrainian Easter eggs, autographs of left handed people, antique tools, etc.

228. Ask your grandparents to tell you tales of their childhoods and family tales *now*. Parents, too.

229. Research your family tree a little (or a lot). It is part of your culture.

230. "Culture" comes from "colere" (Latin) a verb which means to cultivate or to till. The noun, "cultura" means soil cultivation. We are like fields to be enriched and gardened by our teachers, mentors, present experiences, and the past.

231. Learn to make an easy but special dish to take to parties and to potlucks. Make up a tale about the recipe; learn an anecdote about it or the history of some of its ingredients. Even such simple things as bagels, croissants, and pretzels have interesting histories!

232. Visit art, science, natural history, space, and historial museums as frequently as you can.

233. Buy some good stationery for special letters, or put it on your gift list. At times, use it just to feel good about yourself.

234. Learn basic first aid.

235. Learn the Heimlich maneuver.

236. Learn CPR.

237. Learn how to put up a tent by yourself and basic survival techniques, summer and winter.

238. Learn international distress signals.

239. Learn how to keep scores, e.g. baseball box scores, football stats, plus/minus stats for ice hockey, etc.

240. Try fruit and herbal teas, hot or cold, for study sessions.

241. When preparing or taking exams, forget the reputations of the teacher and his tests. Think of the test as *your* chance.

242. Proofread personal letters as you would school work or business projects.

243. Make summer jobs work for you doubly: Earn good pay *and* portfolio/resume potential.

244. Whenever you have worked well on a job for a period of time, ask your boss for a brief note of commendation for your portfolio.

245. People are individuals. Their ideas are part of them. You cannot rightfully take another's idea and claim it as your own anymore than you can claim his eyes or heart.

246. Suggest that one of your organizations or teams plant a small garden on school grounds. Try an easy up-keep herb garden! Better yet, rotate volunteer summer gardeners, and grow veggies for the community food bank.

247. As a club activity, suggest a trash pick-up day on school or community grounds.

248. Think of visits to the doctor, dentist, even the barber as mini-field trips. Be aware of what's going on and learn something! Ask questions!

249. Learn the proper forms of address for speaking and writing to various important people in your lives, ministers, priests, congressmen, etc.

250. School-age children can have huge chalkboards in their rooms made with chalkboard paint. Inquire at your paint dealer's.

251. Taking a puppy to dog training is great kid training! Handling any animal at shows and 4H competitions is highly rewarding.

252. Left handed students may prefer to use the left page to take notes. Extreme lefties may want to use their notebooks from back to front, especially if they habitually go through magazines backwards!

253. From age three on, young people can periodically go through their toys (and later clothing) to discard some items to be given to charity. Before the holidays is an ideal time.

254. Feel free to ask teachers for help and clarification on class work and on tests. You may not get help on tests, but it doesn't hurt to ask.

255. Keep a supply of poster-making materials, rub-on letters, stencils, etc.

256. Check scientific references to see that they are recent and up to date.

257. Write your name and address in all books you own.

258. Memorize frequently used zip codes.

259. Discover the range of study help books: Cliffs Notes, Barron's, Made-Easy books, etc.

260. Memorize common measurements.

261. Learn the background and facts of dance: ballet, ballroom dancing, and various ethnic dances.

263. Research the National Parks and find out the famous attractions in each.

264. Learn about religions other than your own.

265. Get a rhythm in your week to break up monotony. Declare Tuesdays "Grub Day" and Fridays "Dress-up Day." Or, start a breakfast-study group Wednesdays. Be creative and shake up your week.

266. Counselors and teacher confidants are supposed to make you feel good. If you are confiding in one who does not, switch confidants.

267. Counselors and teachers who act as counselors should be working to help you to become independent, not dependent. If you feel you are leaning on a teacher too much, choose another to confide in.

268. Keep a couple of paper bags in your locker to protect things on rainy days and help you carry stuff on busy days.

269. Learn as much as you can about the life and accomplishments of one (at least) artist, musician, architect,

military leader, etc. Make your own list of ten vocations, and research the great practitioners.

270. When you hit an interesting bit of information, plan to dig deeper when you have time. This might be the beginning of later expertise.

271. Cultivate friends of different ages, both younger and older than you.

272. Be a good role model for younger students.

273. Be the kind of young citizen your older neighbors would approve.

274. Be kind to animals; they have much to teach you.

275. Learn something about sign language.

276. Pack a "mental" emergency kit for such disasters as the giggles, test nervousness, or temper. One student cures the giggles by doing math; another calms test nerves by imagining her teacher in funny pajamas.

277. If you need to cry, cry and get it over with. However, practice control so you don't use tears as an immediate, easy reaction to problems.

278. If you have a serious medical problem, make certain the school and all your teachers know about it.

279. Bragging about your successes, clothes, handsomeness, or allowance is an eloquent display of your insecurity.

280. Bragging about your parents' success or money is worse.

281. Most folks dislike nosey people.

282. Never discuss the details of your love life with friends.

283. Be alert to bad days that the teachers are having. Then be a friend, and help by being quiet or helping class discussion run smoothly.

284. Help friends do their work, and suggest they study; but if they ask for answers only, tell them you have a policy against giving answers out.

285. If you are seriously interested in a subject such as chess or astronomy, ecology or animal rights, ask a suitable teacher/sponsor to help you found a club. One of my students founded a Newcomers' Club for the school.

286. A good source of summer work is a teacher-run business, especially if he knows you.

287. Never, ever, say you turned in work when you did not.

288. If you need an extension of a deadline, always ask the teacher as much in advance as is possible.

289. Understand when a teacher gives you a definite "No," and work around it as best you can.

290. Most libraries now offer interesting brochures on a number of things: New books, meetings, services, and book groups.

291. Self-help books (like *Super Student*) have good ideas. Choose which ones best suit you.

292. Memorize significant lines from poetry you like. Quoting such elevated thought is inspiring, impressive, and fresh. You'll win fans.

293. Playfully kid kids. No heavy teasing. It's intellectual play, and nothing is more fun.

294. Write famous people who interest you. They may respond!

295. Try to tackle some small segment of history with a life-long effort, e. g. learning the *real* rules to old childhood games, famous left-handed people, or the history of various foods.

296. Invent jokes. Create puns. Fill your speech with playful ironic twists while keeping a straight face.

297. Add a volume of American folksongs to your library whether or not you are musical. Study lyrics and histories.

298. When taking tests with printed answer sheets, always, always check that your questions are properly aligned with the answer sheets.

299. Guard against over-reacting to bad grades. Analyze the situation; resolve to improve weaknesses; and put the grade behind you.

300. When you suffer a tragedy or trauma, talk it over as soon as possible with mature people--teachers or parents.

301. There is a wide range of non-perishable healthy snacks, like fruit and granola bars. Keep some in your book bag or locker.

302. Make certain the messages on your T-shirts are inoffensive.

303. Keep sexy clothes out of the classroom.

304. Report emotional abuse from teachers as quickly as you would report physical abuse.

305. Report abuse, physical, sexual, or emotional, among students to a counselor, principal, or the police.

306. If you find school authorities are not responding to your problem, discuss it thoroughly with your parents, and request that the superintendent or, if necessary, the School Board be informed.

307. Make sure you fill out all school information cards completely and accurately with addresses, phone numbers, and doctor's names, and keep them up to date.

308. While breaks and playground time are for exercise, you might be in the mood to just rest quietly and smell spring or fall in the air. That's good for the soul!

309. If someone takes something you've said the wrong way, apologize for the misunderstanding as if it *were* your fault.

310. It is best not to comment on anyone's weight, one way or another.

311. Realize that playing school politics is not only a waste of time, but a pursuit empty of worth.

312. Avoid angry people.

313. Remember that prejudice means "pre-judge."

314. Try new foods, at least twice.

315. Get a pen pal, or carry on a correspondence with a friend.

316. Get one notebook in which to engage a friend in a dialog on a subject of mutual interest: music, books, films, tropical fish, etc.

317. Get a good pair of scissors, and don't lose them.

318. Sleep with a window open, at least a crack.

319. Start a savings account.

320. Write a letter to your newspaper when you care about an issue.

321. Read a news magazine weekly--at least the headlines. Younger children should ask parents to find newspapers which have special children's pages.

322. Everyone should have at least one magazine subscription.

323. Start to address envelopes with your pen at the center. Check letter form in a book.

324. Learn the correct way to fold paper for a standard envelope (4 1/8" x 9 1/2"): in thirds, bottom up (covering signature), top third down.

325. Everyone should learn to cook a simple meal, a killer hamburger, or perhaps a special sandwich.

326. Help foreign exchange students, and learn by doing so.

327. Don't wear heavy fragrances from cosmetic or hygiene products to class.

328. Periodically, think something good and turn the thought into a smile. Feel your facial muscles lighten up.

329. Most people are reluctant to loan personal items, e. g. a hair brush or a shirt. Think before you ask.

330. Buy a copy of a favorite book and keep it handy in your locker or backpack to read.

331. Write "Thank you" notes for gifts. Say something *specific* about the particular gift, e. g. "Fuchsia is my favorite color." or "I really needed the $5 right now!"

332. Get to know people in professions that interest you. Visit them (as their time allows) at their places of work, if possible.

333. Support your community and your larger community, your country.

334.   Have personal cards made for business or social exchange. Some malls have machines which will make a set for $5.00.

335.   Make a "wish list" of books and scholarly equipment. When someone asks, "What do you want for a birthday (or holiday)?"-- you're ready with suggestions.

336.   A little serious exercise is good preparation for a long study session.

337.   High schoolers might try studying together the night before a big test. However, get home early enough to do your final review alone.

338.   Don't wear shirts or sweats with slogans printed in the negative. "Save the Earth" is positive. "Down with Pollution" is negative.

339.   If you are shy, make it a point to say hello to other people. Set a goal such as "Hellos" to three people when passing to class in the hall.

340. Monitor your voice. Periodically, concentrate on listening to how you sound. Is your voice too loud or soft? Are you speaking at a reasonable rate? Is your voice too shrill? Too nasal?

341.   Never, ever "Boo" teams, yours or theirs, at sporting events.

342. Good conversation starter/ice breaker: "What's the good word in math?" "Or art?" Or, "What kind of jokes is Mr. Parks telling now?"

343. Keeping a journal (a record of daily reflections) is a better stress buster than keeping a diary (a records of events).

344. Developing a good set of telephone manners pays off very well!

345. Learn the reputations of the various periodicals. Are they liberal or conservative? Produced for a mass audience or a smaller group of intellectuals?

346. Learn the abbreviations for various degrees, e. g. Ph. D., M. D., O. D., etc., and what the qualifications are for each.

347. Learn all the interesting processes in life: how to make cheese, wine, beer, and potting soil and pesto!

348. You don't have to be an antique buff, but keep something old and meaningful in your belongings to remind you of the legacy of the past.

349. Look through a good food magazine now and then (*Gourmet, Bon Appetit*, etc.). The quality of the writing is superb.

350. Give yourself personal goals. Consider what you think you can do confidently, and boost that level a bit.

351. Many, many opportunities take only a little time and effort and a postage stamp. Write letters to open doors. The results will surprise you.

352. Get to know one opera. Know the story, who played the parts famously, a little about the composer and his period, and listen, listen, listen to it. This might lead to a life-long love.

353. Discover foreign films. Subtitles improve reading, and they are wonderful aids to foreign language students.

354. Don't miss the chance to see foreign animated films, i.e. cartoons. The vastly different animation styles of various countries give incredible insight into their cultures.

355. Be a good neighbor at your locker, in your community.

356. Learn dog jokes, cat jokes, profession jokes, and as many puns as you can! Practice telling these.

357. Try to find a joke that depends upon body language and/or gesticulation, if not actual acting roles or mime. Perfect it alone, and save performances for very special occasions.

358. Don't experiment with anything--sex, drugs, or sky-diving until you know all the mechanics and medical facts, and have learned about them from a *reliable* source.

359. Check out a book of common foreign expressions. Learn a few *bon mots* to fill your speech with *joie de vivre!*

360. Listen to public radio and public TV (if any TV at all!).

361. Support the arts. Brainstorm ways you can do this according to your budget.

362. Learn a skill involving your hands, whether or not you can master it, or even become good at it. Anyone can, at the least, learn the basics of knitting, woodworking (carpentry), painting, bread making, whittling, etc.

363. Learn about knots, the kinds of knots, types of nautical knots, the names and history of knots. Bonus: Know how to tie them. Find *Ashley's Book of Knots* in a library or bookstore.

364. Have an interview/dress-up/performance outfit ready to go in your closet. Have it in mind mentally and clean to wear on a moment's notice.

365. Don't forget school events that are important to your classmates and teachers, although not especially to you. Check the school calendar.

366. Do a good deed daily, and don't tell anyone about it.

367. Ask to obtain and support a bird feeder. Watch it.

368. Read a good book on animal intelligence. It will give you much insight into human behavior. Try Stanley Coren's *The Intelligence of Dogs*.

369. Greet someone you don't know well in the hall. Even a friendly nod is a positive gesture.

370. The preposition "with" goes with comparisons (likenesses); the preposition "to" goes with contrasts (differences). For instance, I compare the coolness of ice cream *with* the coolness of yogurt.   I contrast 18th century science *to* that of the 19th century.

371. Stay out of the teacher's desk, grade book, and attendance book unless invited.

372. Using *irregardless* is substandard English. Actually is it a double negative, IRregardLESS.

373. Keep the names and addresses of former teachers. You may want to check something from their classes. You may want a recommendation.

374. Use recycled paper for obvious reasons. Doing so is a class act.

375. If you must sell stuff to raise funds for school activities, use the experience to practice selling skills. Don't just beg for money.

376. Sometimes try to work with groups that are mainly of the opposite sex. This is a good democratic practice, and (Yeah!) it's fun.

377. For thoughtful discussion, avoid asking questions which can be answered with "yes" or "no." It is better to use words like "explain," "evaluate," "prove," etc.

378. Don't neglect books because they are above or below your reading level or age. There are treasures in children's literature. Many adults love to read good kids' stuff. (How did Speilberg make *E. T.* ?) You can gain self-esteem from looking at art books and browsing in books about Old English or theoretical physics.

379. Learn how to read maps, charts, and graphs.

380. Analyze and evaluate comedians. Find your favorite, and know why!

381. Make one phone call a day in which there's something for someone else, not you! Perhaps a tip, a compliment, or some helpful information?

382: Write one letter a week, minimum--even if it is sending away for a freebie or writing your congressman.

383. Vote. Vote in a simple show of hands in class, in school elections, and in local and national elections when you are old enough.

384. Be confident! Vote for yourself.

385. Computer literate students should practice and show their skills as much as they can. They should use them in their portfolios, for instance.

386. Go all out when tackling math and science. Make your study area conducive to these subjects with Escher and Einstein posters, good equipment. Use a good calculator, your own copies of your texts (Ask your teacher to help you order.), proper papers, and writing instruments. Treat math and science like big time! They are.

387. To encourage independence, teens might read Emerson's *Self Reliance* and Thoreau's *Walden*. Young readers might read *The Secret Garden*.

388. Take an idea from journalism. Keep a morgue (SEE SCHOOL SUPPLIES.) Keep this separate notebook for your ideas, your musings, a list of things you want to look up or

investigate later. Keep a running "intellectual/academic shopping list." A morgue is your creative store--as Cole Porter said, "Anything goes!"

389. Lighten up, and learn how to laugh at your own expense; and never, *ever*, laugh at anyone else's.

390. Sending a note to a principal commending a teacher's work is the highest of compliments.

391. Let your teacher know how you like to work--alone, in groups, sitting or working at the board.

392. Good listeners are rare; they are the best of friends.

393. Consider doing nothing as a possible "course of action" when you are in a real dilemma.

394. A punch, index cards, and three inch metal rings available at office supply stores make an innovative handy vocabulary ring. Use them for math and science theorems, too.

395. Discount stores have excellent posters for the study area of your room. Consider motivational posters such as those in classrooms, sports posters which suggest drive and success, or good art--art that makes you think!

396. Don't give up your family's religion, politics, or traditions unless you have something *proven* better to replace them.

397. Christian or not, review the fourth commandment. That's the one about honoring your mother and father.

398. Find your talents, discover your possibilities, and cherish them through use.

399. Love and cherish the earth. Look up the word "stewardship."

400. "Love yourself" translates into "Respect yourself."

About the author...

Sally Ketchum has worked with super students and happy kids from kindergarteners to college students. Ketchum loves children, animals, and nature. She enjoys cooking, gardening (herbs, perennials, and roses), reading, writing, and wilderness island camping in Lake Michigan. A graduate of The University of Michigan, she is the mother of three adult children and the mistress of three super and happy dogs.

Use the form below to order additional copies of
Super Student/Happy Kid!.
Ship to: (Please print.)
Name: _____
Address: _____
City, State, Zip _____
Phone: _____

__ copies of *Super Student/Happy Kid!* @ $.9.95 each $____
Postage and handling @ $1.25 per book $____
Michigan residents add 6% tax $____
Total amount enclosed $____
Make checks payable to Summer Island Press
Send to: P. O. Box 279
Williamsburg, MI 49690-0279
Call (616) 267-5786 for discount information on bulk sales.

Use the form below to order additional copies of
Super Student/Happy Kid!
Ship to: (Please print.)
Name: _____
Address: _____
City, State, Zip _____
Phone: _____

__ copies of *Super Student/Happy Kid!* @ $9.95 each $____
Postage and handling @ $1.25 per book $____
Michigan residents add 6% tax $____
Total amount enclosed $____
Make checks payable to Summer Island Press
Send to: P. O. Box 279
Williamsburg, MI 49690-0279
Call (616) 267-5786 for discount information on bulk sales.

If you enjoyed *Super Student/Happy Kid!* and have tips which you would like to contribute to *Super Student/Happy Kid!--volume II,* fill in the form below and mail to:

Super Student/Happy Kid!
P. O. Box 279
Williamsburg, MI 49690-0279

We'll send you a free copy of 100 New Red Hot Tips for your suggestions. Further, all comments on *Super Student* are welcome!

Name:
_____

Address:
_____

_____

Phone:
_____

I give permission for you to use my tip and/or comment.

(Signature) _____

Red Hot Tip (Attach page if you wish.)
_____
_____
_____
_____

Comment on Book:
_____
_____
_____